The Ghost Gloucestershire

Keith Clark

REDCLIFFE
Bristol

First published in 1993 by
Redcliffe Press Ltd
49 Park St, Bristol.

© *Keith Clark*
Cover photograph: *Jack Tait*

ISBN 1 872971 28 8

British Cataloguing-in-Publication Data.
A catalogue record for this book is available
from the British Library.

Typeset and printed by
The Longdunn Press Ltd., Bristol.

Introduction

It sometimes seems that when the sun goes down in Gloucestershire the night air fills with gliding ladies, headless horsemen, spectral soldiers from every period and clanking chains.

Can there be a county in England that has as many ghosts and other supernatural forms as Gloucestershire?

This book is a collection of recorded sightings and what are perhaps no more than legends. As to the nature of what people may or may not have seen, I leave that to the reader to decide.

I would like to thank all those who have helped me, including the ever helpful staff of Gloucester, Cheltenham and Bristol libraries and the various sources from which I have quoted.

In particular I would like to express my gratitude to all those very sensible, rational, ordinary people who told me about their own personal encounter with something that so many experts have tried to explain but for most of us remains firmly outside our understanding.

Keith Clark

Garden Reach

We all know what a haunted house looks like. It is a rambling, run-down Gothic manor, with bats flying around the tower and the occasional candlelit shadow passing in front of an upstairs window. It has a huge oak door that creaks open by itself to reveal a baronial hall, complete with suits of armour, cobwebs and a portrait of an evil looking man in period dress over the fireplace.

Meanwhile, outside, the mist is starting to swirl across the overgrown garden to the family tomb in the neighbouring graveyard . . .

That's the haunted houses as portrayed in countless films and comics. It's an image far removed from reality, and bears no similarity at all to one of the most celebrated haunted houses in Britain – a quiet and stately Victorian house in the elegant spa town of Cheltenham.

St Anne's, on the corner of Pittville Circus Road and All Saints Road, is now made up of flats, but it was originally built as a single Victorian house called Garden Reach. It doesn't look any different from hundreds of other houses of its period in the town. Nor did it actually suffer from any spectacular haunting.

There were no headless horsemen riding up and down the stairs, no troops of ghostly soldiers or chain dragging monks in the living room, just a lady dressed in black holding a handkerchief up to her face.

What made the ghost of Garden Reach so interesting was that one of the occupants of the house kept notes of every encounter with the lady in black. These she made available to psychic experts who were able to investigate the house and its history and talk to reliable witnesses. As one expert said at the time, Garden Reach became one of the best authenticated cases on record and it still features in most serious books on the subject.

The house was built on a market garden in the 1860s and even before it was completed it had been bought. Its first owners were solicitor Henry Swinhoe and his wife Elizabeth. Sadly, Elizabeth died within a few years, aged only 35, leaving Henry with four young children, two girls and two boys. He was, by all accounts, devastated by the death of his wife and took to drinking heavily.

Four years later though, in 1870, he remarried. His second wife,

Imogen, thought she could cure him of his drinking, but eventually she too sought solace in the bottle and Garden Reach became the setting for numerous violent rows and scenes, often about the children for whom Imogen seems to have been something of a tyrannical stepmother.

Henry Swinhoe's second marriage only lasted a short time; in 1876, Imogen left him and moved to Clifton, Bristol. Henry died in July the same year. She outlived him by only two years, dying on September 23rd, 1878, aged only 41 years. The cause of her death was dipsomania and subacute gastritis.

Strangely, considering she had moved away, Imogen instructed in her will that she was to be buried in Holy Trinity Church, Portland Street, just a few yards from Garden Reach.

After the Swinhoes, the house was bought by an elderly couple who renamed it Pittville Hall, but in just a few months the husband had died, his wife had moved out and the house was sold.

The new owner only lived in it for a few months and when he moved out it remained empty for four years. Could he perhaps not sell or rent it out in that time because it had now become a haunted house?

In April 1882, however, the owner found a tenant, Captain F. W. Despard who moved in with his invalid wife and their six children Rosina, Edith, Henry, William, Mabel and Wilfred. Their 26 year old married daughter was also a regular visitor. They renamed the house Donore.

It was Rosina Despard who first saw the ghost and sent regular details of the haunted happenings to a friend, Catherine Campbell, in the north of England. Her correspondent, with Rosina's permission, sent these notes to the Society for Psychical Research.

The story was investigated by Frederick W. H. Myers, honorary secretary and one of the founders of the Society. He had relatives living nearby and was able to question many of the witnesses in person.

His researches and Rosina Despard's notes were published in the Society's *Proceedings* (vol VIII). This was in turn reprinted in *The Cheltenham Ghost* (Psychic Press 1948), a book devoted to Garden Reach written by B. Abdy Collins, editor of the journal *Psychic Science.*

Rosina Despard was 19 when she had her first encounter with the ghost in June 1882:

The figure was that of a tall lady, dressed in black of a soft woollen material, judging from the slight sound in moving. The face was hidden by a handkerchief held in the right hand. This is all I noticed then, but on further occasions, when I was able to observe her more closely, I saw the upper part of the left side of the forehead, and a little of the hair above. Her left hand was hidden by her sleeve and a fold of her dress. As she held it down a portion of a widow's cuff was visible on both wrists, so that the whole impression was that of a lady in widow's weeds. There was no cap on the head but a general effect of blackness suggests a bonnet, with a long veil or a hood.

Over the next few years, Rosina Despard, various members of the family, servants and visitors all saw the tall lady. Strangely, neither Captain nor Mrs Despard ever saw her even though the other members of the family stated that she was often seen in the same room as them. She was seen walking around the house, seated at a writing desk and even in the garden during daylight.

Rosina tried several times to photograph her but with no success. She also attempted to make physical contact; 'It was not that there was nothing to touch but that she always seemed to be beyond me . . .'

On one occasion a group of the children made a circle around the ghost but it just walked between two of them and disappeared. Rosina tried tying threads across the top of the stairs to trap the ghost but this also did not prove any obstacle to the ghost who just glided through them.

It seems likely that the tall lady in black was Imogen Swinhoe.

Captain Despard discovered that a local carpenter had been employed by Henry Swinhoe to fix a secret box beneath the floorboards of the Morning Room in which he placed Elizabeth's jewellery, presumably to keep them from his second wife. Despard traced the carpenter who showed him the box beneath the floor, but it was now empty.

It has been suggested that Imogen Swinhoe was still looking for the jewels, which may explain the fact that the one room in which the ghost was never seen was the Morning Room.

During the earlier sightings, the ghost had a very strong, solid appearance. One witness, not a member of the family, said that the figure passed close to her and she didn't realise it was not an ordinary woman. Over the years, it grew more and more indistinct until in 1889 it seems to have given up its search and stopped appearing.

The Despards left the house in 1893 and in subsequent years

Garden Reach as it is today. In the 19th century it was haunted by a lady in black.

7

Garden Reach had numerous changes of owner and name. It was a boys' preparatory school, it was owned by an order of nuns, it became St Anne's Nursing College and the property of the Diocese of Gloucester. In 1973 a housing association converted it into flats.

The hauntings did not stop however. There were occasional sightings right up to the 1920s when one report said that boys in the town used to go to the house to see 'the ghost dancing across the lawn.'

Since then, the house appears to have been at peace. However, in 1961 two men saw a woman in black, wearing a bonnet and with a handkerchief held to her face, in the house opposite (Cotswold Lodge, since demolished). And in January 1970 a learner driver in this part of the town saw a woman in black with a handkerchief held to her face – but the instructor could see nothing.

Perhaps Imogen Swinhoe, unable to find the jewellery in Garden Reach, has decided to search further afield?

Slowwe House, Arlingham

An exorcism is usually carried out to rid a house of a ghost or spirit. This can take many different forms, from a religious service carried out by a clergyman to trapping the unwelcomed guest in a sealed container which is buried or, as at Burford, thrown in the river.

It doesn't always work, however, as was discovered by the occupants of Slowwe House in Arlingham.

Slowwe House dates back to the 14th century, when it was a small, one storey thatched cottage but over the centuries bits have been added to it – a Victorian wing, Gothic windows, a Jacobean staircase etc – and today it is a rambling three storey building.

The site on which is stands goes back even further. The courtyard is probably Roman, there's a Roman coffin in the garden and at the bottom of the garden is a monastery wall. There is a tiny chapel attached to one side of the house.

In the 1960s, Slowwe House was occupied by hippies, but a ghost gave one of them such a bad time that he eventually called in a priest to hold an exorcism.

Despite this, the ghost of a lady in grey continued to be seen around the house.

There has been no explanation as to the identity of the grey lady or why she haunted this house.

Janet and Don Lacey bought the back wing of the house in 1970, moving with their seven children into the barn opposite while renovation work was being carried out. It was from the barn that Mrs Lacey first saw the grey lady.

'I looked down into the courtyard one day and saw her walking across,' she explained to the *Gloucester Journal* (July 15th, 1986) 'She had on a long grey dress and a grey bonnet. I did a double take but she was still there. When I looked again she had gone.'

Mrs Lacey went on to tell the reporter that after she saw it in the kitchen and on the landing, the ghost seemed particularly interested in one of the bedrooms, where their daughters had woken up to see the lady watching them.

Lights kept being turned on and off, windows were opened and shut and pictures kept falling off the walls.

'One night we came over to the house from the barn to switch off the lights three times. And I got so fed up of picking up one picture that I eventually decided to leave it down'.

She went on to tell the *Journal*, 'Before I came to live here I was as sceptical as the next person about ghosts. But, now I have seen her three times and my children have seen her too, I believe.'

In the 18th century, the occupants of the Court House in Arlingham also had good reason to believe in the supernatural. On May 24th, 1757, they saw a ghostly funeral making its way up the avenue towards the house. Exactly 12 months later, the death took place of John Yate, the last male heir of the family who owned the Court House.

Alice Godfrey, who documented many personal ghost sightings in the county at the turn of the century, had an unnerving experience when she visited Arlingham church on June 18th, 1902 to see some carvings.

Sitting in the left hand front pew was a lady, dressed in a black gown, white lace cap and her hair in a bun. When Alice asked her for the whereabouts of the carvings, the lady just looked at her, smiled and vanished.

As she left the church, Alice turned round and looked back – and the old lady had returned to her seat. She asked a gardener tending the churchyard about the lady: 'That's old Mrs Budge; she was the vicar's housekeeper,' she was told, 'She's been dead for many a year now.'

The Ageing Hand

A normal looking semi-detached house in Chapen Street in the popular Cotswold village of Stow-on-the-Wold was subjected to a whole host of poltergeist activity during 1963 and 1964.

According to published reports, pools of water began appearing in different parts of the house and water streamed up walls. The owners, Mr and Mrs Pethick, called in three plumbers but they could not find any leaks or anything else to explain this phenomenon. There were also tapping sounds from inside cupboards, writing on the wall and a voice of a man claiming to be the builder of the house who had died 20 years earlier.

In one of the bedrooms, their 14 year old son experienced something that sounds as horrifying as any scene from a Stephen King story. He was thrown out of bed, sheets were ripped, the headboard to the bed was gouged. And worse still, a hand appeared at the bottom of the bed and slowly aged from a child's to that of a man.

The family went on holiday to Devon, but there was no respite, for the ghost decided to go with them!

Fortunately for the Pethick family, whatever it was that was accompanying them took a liking to the local church and the vicar there and decided to stay.

When they returned to Stow, it was to enjoy living in Chapen Street without any more trouble.

Old Bell, Dursley

Spend the night in Room 6 at the Old Bell Hotel in Long Street, Dursley, and you sleep in a bedroom where a young chambermaid hanged herself. And you may experience some of the strange things that have happened here.

One person who stayed in Room 6 in 1970 was Geoffrey McEwan from Wallsend-on-Tyne. He had an appointment the next morning and asked for an early call.

He was woken by a voice outside his door, 'It is eight o'clock.' He didn't get up straightaway but dozed for a few minutes. 'It is eight-fifteen,' said the same voice outside the door. He went downstairs for breakfast but there didn't seem to be anyone around. It was then that he saw the clock. It was three-fifteen in the morning.

The story was confirmed to the *Gloucestershire County Gazette* (October 9th, 1971) by Tom Creed, manager of the Lloyds Bank branch in Dursley who was staying at The Old Bell at the time and had spoken to Mr McEwan.

'I remember he was going for an interview at Mawdsleys that day. He said someone woke him up saying it was eight o'clock. He said he went down the stairs but the time was only 3am.

'I said he might have dreamt it because he was having an interview next day. It was the night of the 12th day of Christmas.'

Mr McEwan did not stay for the interview, and it seems he hurriedly left Dursley – and who can blame him?

On another occasion, William Lloyd, landlord of the Old Bell at the time of Mr McEwan's visit, was in the kitchen with his wife Sylvia when the old fashioned call bell rang from Room 6. The bell was not connected.

The 15th century inn has had such a rich history, you would be surprised if it didn't have at least one ghost.

The dining room was used as an Assize Court in which at least two people were sentenced to death. In 1680 a murder was committed in one of the rooms.

And there was Annie, a chambermaid at the turn of the century, who hanged herself in Room Six when she became pregnant and her soldier lover refused to marry her.

Clairvoyant Mrs Marie Dykes told the *Gazette* that she had felt someone was in the dining room:

'I turned round and there was a girl standing in the doorway. She had a long dress on and something dangling down – but I don't know what it was. I think it was a chain. She did not speak. I said "Can I help you?" She beckoned me forward, and she made for the stairs. But when I got to the bottom of the stairs she had

11

The Old Bell Hotel in Dursley, where numerous hauntings have been reported.

disappeared. I knew she was a ghost because of the way she glided along.'

Interestingly, she did not mind going into Rooms 6 and 7 but said that Room 9 was also haunted 'and it feels terrible to go in there.'

Black Horse, Cirencester

The haunting of the 15th century Black Horse in Castle Street, Cirencester, in 1933 has been well documented thanks to a series of articles in a local newspaper.

Around midnight on August 13th, 1933, Ruth Bower, the landlord's niece, woke up to see an evil looking old lady in a fawn-coloured silk dress, apron and mop cap in her room. Not surprisingly, she screamed and the ghost vanished through the wall.

Miss Bower remembered that in the strange glow that surrounded the spectre, the room had looked different. She could clearly see the window in the outside wall, despite the fact that a partition had recently been built to form a passage between her room and the wall.

When her uncle and aunt searched the room, they found that a name, *James* had been scratched, upside down, into one of the window panes.

The Vale of the White Horse Gazette (August 18th, 1933) covered the story in great detail:

> Disbelievers would say that the writing on the window was there before Sunday – the night of the ghost's visitation – but the landlord of the hotel is confident that it was not there previously. Since he and his wife had frequently cleaned the window in question, it is inconceivable that they would not have noticed it.
>
> Apparently the scratches formed part of an attempt to cut a signature into the glass and, curiously enough, the scratching is obviously new – not having assumed the dark appearance common to cuts that have been in glass for some time.

The enterprising *Gazette* reporter returned to The Black Horse accompanied by a Mrs X, an unnamed medium said to have had no knowledge of the inn or even where it stood.

The report of August 25th tells us that when the medium arrived

13

in Castle Street she stopped and stated that the party was not alone but surrounded by people in brown and white cowls.

At the inn she was able to tell the landlady where the original entrance had been many years before and various alterations that had been made inside the building, all of which Mrs Bower was able to confirm.

In their journey around the house, the medium refused to enter a ground floor room and the two rooms above it, and on entering a bedroom the reporter told his readers:

> She seemed to wither, her back bowed and her left leg was twisted inwards. The fingers of her right hand twisted and grasped some strange object. Her voice was that of an old woman. Her words came slowly. 'I feel sad,' she murmured, 'very, very sad. I have a terrible pain in my leg. I cannot walk properly. I have a stick in my hand. I tap on the floor with it.'
>
> Still limping Mrs X went from room to room until she finally straightened her back and became almost 'her normal self' although throughout the rest of the proceedings she was unable to straighten her leg and the foot was twisted into a grotesque position.

Strangely her return to her normal self took place in the haunted room occupied by Miss Bower.

According to Mrs X, the story she was getting from the house was that the old lady had caused some injury to an old man who lived with her in the house. It was not in the niece's room though but in one of the rooms she refused to enter.

The story was kept alive by the *Gazette* and its correspondents for a number of weeks and in September Mrs X returned to the inn where she entered the Number 3 bedroom, which she had previously been unable to enter.

Facing a wall, she told the landlord that she saw two windows – this was not possible to the normal eye because a partition built some years before to divide the room into a bedroom and bathroom, hid them from view.

She then laid three white flowers there in a form of short exorcism, which partially seems to have worked for the evil-looking old lady has only subsequently been seen on two known occasions.

Sadly, in 1992, the frame around the window rotted away and the window fell out and was completely smashed. The present manager, Malcolm Collins, told me that local people expect that the name will re-appear on one of the new panes, 'We are all waiting for it to come back, but if it does I'm moving out'.

Anglian Windows, Gloucester

On the night of Hallowe'en, 1988, two men agreed to stay overnight in the much haunted offices of Anglian Windows in Westgate Street, Gloucester, as part of a fund-raising scheme.

Severn Sound radio had earlier installed equipment in a locked room so that the two could broadcast live on radio.

When Steve Pugh and Robin Ledbury arrived for their vigil, they found the door still locked but inside the room all the radio equipment had been disturbed and wires pulled out. Bravely they went on with their plan and throughout the night recorded and broadcast a series of crashes and bangs, a table being turned over, lights being switched on and off.

Earlier that year, Mrs Jean Brown, who worked in the Anglian showroom, told the publication *Source* (August, 11th, 1988) of how eight members of staff had all seen a carpet lift itself up as if there was someone underneath it, and a host of other unexplained incidents.

This was followed by the sighting of a robed man in the showroom and a hand basin being thrown down the stairs.

In September, medium Phillip Seff was called in and held a seance, attended by journalists and photographers.

During the seance, Seff made contact with a man with long white hair and a beard, wearing a grey robe, who had broken his neck and died after falling from the building.

One of the two men who spent the night in the building, café owner Steve Pugh, had had an earlier experience of the ghost, so he knew something of what to expect.

Working in his café he heard a crash and breaking glass from an upstairs window of the Anglian building. Inside, in a locked and bolted room, he and office manager Jean Brown discovered that a large wardrobe had mysteriously been pushed into a window, scattering glass into Bull Lane.

Seff held a second seance in the building just prior to the vigil, this time the 'monk-like' person told him that he was searching for a key he'd lost in there.

Ghosts Of The Civil War

The Civil War ended with the execution of Charles I in 1649. But throughout Gloucestershire, scene of so many battles and skirmishes between the supporters of the Crown and the Parliamentarians, ghostly Cavaliers still roam the lanes and haunt the cellars and landings of old houses.

A cavalier knocks at the door of The Angel Inn in the Forest of Dean town of Coleford, for instance, while a few miles away, in Newland, a whole troop of Royal soldiers were seen.

The porter of the King's Head in Cirencester must have had a nasty shock when a ghostly cavalier pulled out his flintlock pistol and shot at him. This, says local legend, may be from an incident in 1688 when Lord Lovelace was attacked by Stuart supporters in the Market Place and one of his companions, Bulstrode Whitelock, was shot and taken to the King's Head where he died from his wounds.

As in any war, communication was most important to both sides and despatch riders and messengers criss-crossed the country during the Civil War with news of the fighting and orders to officers on the field.

A Royalist messenger travelling from Sudeley to Gloucester was brought down from his horse at Prestbury by a rope strung across the road and summarily executed. Considering that Prestbury has very good claim to be the most haunted town in England, it is not surprising to find the rider's ghost is still here.

The ghost of a despatch rider from an earlier war also still haunts the people of Prestbury. He dates from 1471, the time of The War of the Roses, and it is thought that he was taking news of the battle at Worcester to Gloucester. He was shot by a single arrow and was buried on the spot. The discovery of a skeleton of a man with an arrow in his rib cage, uncovered during road works in Shaw Green Lane, gives some credence to the story.

It is not just the Cavaliers who have stayed on in Gloucestershire in spectral form. The screams and shouts of a group of Parliamen-

16

tarians have been heard at Aust, near the Severn Bridge, where they were drowned after being tricked by the ferryman, a Royalist supporter.

They forced the ferryman to take them across, but he put them off not quite on the other side, but on rocks that only jut out of the river at low tide. Knowing the ways of the Severn, he was able to get away before the treacherous tide surged over the rock and drowned them.

Roundheads have also been seen in Whitecliff, near Coleford, and local tradition has it that Oliver Cromwell haunts Starvall Farm near Stow-on-the-Wold, where he was refused grain for his horses.

On April 24th, 1644, Parliament soldiers attacked Littledean Hall and captured 20 soldiers in the guardhouse. A few private soldiers were inside the house and one of them shot a Roundhead trooper. In the skirmish that followed, the Roundheads killed Colonel Congreve, governor of Newnham, and Captain Wigmore who was in charge of the garrison. They were killed inside the house and their blood for many years stained the floor, despite the boards being scrubbed and even planed.

When Gloucester was under siege, the Roundheads under Colonel Massey set all the buildings close to the city walls alight so they couldn't be used as cover by the besieging troops. A young boy and his mother were unable to flee their home and were burnt to death. They have continued to haunt the site on which their house stood.

A rather sad Romeo and Juliet style story from the Civil War is associated with Goodrich Castle, just across the River Wye. It tells of two young lovers from opposite sides of the conflict. On the Royalist side was a young Cavalier, Charles Clifford, based inside the castle; on the other, Alice Birch, the daughter of Colonel Birch who was leading the Parliamentary forces besieging the castle.

Alice, obviously a determined young woman, managed to cross the lines and to join her Cavalier lover in the castle. When the castle was surrendered they escaped on horseback through the Roundhead lines to the Wye.

The storm that had helped them make their escape unnoticed had, unfortunately, caused the river to swell and the young lovers were drowned trying to make the crossing. Their cries can sometimes be heard above the noise of the rushing river on stormy nights.

Eddel's Revenge

In the days before the Saxon invasion, part of Gloucestershire was ruled over by a British chieftain by the name of Eddel.

When the Saxons reached the West, they invited Eddel and 460 of his followers to a feast. It did not end in the way that the Britons had expected. They were set upon by their Saxon hosts and every one of them was killed – all, that is, except Eddel.

In true heroic fashion, he grabbed a hedge stake and defended himself by swinging it around like a club, killing 70 Saxons before escaping into Cranham woods.

Some years later, Eddel secretly returned to Gloucestershire and Cranham, but fell ill. A man named Eppa, skilled in healing, was called to treat him, but gave him a fatal distillation of poison instead of medicine!

According to legend, Eddel was buried at the top of a hill behind the Royal William by the path leading up through the woods. The mound is known as Eddel's Tump and his ghost is said to haunt this part of the woods and the lane near Eddel's Mill.

Is he perhaps still seeking revenge for his 460 followers killed by the cowardly deceit of the Saxons at that feast?

A Black Night For Sir Roger

Poor Beatrice still waits for her highwayman lover, cruelly trapped and murdered by her brothers at Dovers Hill.

Beatrice and brothers John and Maurice were Puritans and followers of the Parliamentarian cause. Near neighbour, Sir Roger, fought on the Royalist side.

After Charles I's execution and the rise of Cromwell and the Commonwealth, Sir Roger, like so many other young Cavaliers, was forced to turn to crime to make a living. He became a highwayman, nicknamed The Black Knight.

Beatrice was a passenger in one of the coaches that he challenged to stop. His mask was no disguise, for she had known him since childhood and recognised his voice.

They fell in love and arranged to meet at the foot of Dovers Hill, scene of the famous Cotswold Olympic Games, on the first evening after the full moon.

Knowing that her brothers would be angry, she used to let Sir Roger know that the coast was clear by waving her white silk cloak as a signal.

But their secret was discovered and Beatrice was sent away to stay with relatives while John and Maurice planned to trap her lover.

Taking her white cloak they lay in wait for Sir Roger at the lovers' meeting place at the foot of Dovers Hill. Soon they heard his approach, they waved the cloak and Sir Roger fell into their trap and was slain.

When she heard what had happened, Beatrice lost her mind and was committed to an asylum where she spent the rest of her days.

A kindly nurse allowed her to wear her white cloak on the first evening after a full moon. Which she still does as she waits for her Black Knight at the foot of Dovers Hill.

The Upset Teacher

The College of Technology annexe in Archdeacon Street, off Westgate Street, Gloucester, is a resource centre for teachers, but it was originally built in 1852 as a school.

During alterations in 1968, the decorators used the headmaster's office beneath the main stairs as a store-room. One morning when they unlocked the office, they were dumb-struck to discover that tins of paint had been mysteriously spilled.

The caretaker was hit by a shovel in the empty boiler room, lights were mysteriously turned on and the children began seeing an old man with white hair wearing a gown and mortar board, whom they christened Charlie.

Eventually the school called in J. A. Brooks, author of *Ghosts and Witches of the Cotswolds*, who held a seance at the school on Midsummer Night's Eve.

He successfully made contact with the ghost who told him that he had taught at the school a long time ago. In too much of a hurry he had run down the stairs, slipped and tragically injured himself. He was carried to the headmaster's study, the room in which the paint was spilled, and had died there.

The presence of the builders had upset him, he told the seance, and he had spilled the paint to frighten them. He hadn't, he told Brooks, wanted to harm the caretaker but was just trying to pass the shovel.

When the alterations were completed, the master's ghost quietened down again, although there have been some occasional unexplained incidents in the building.

Rolling Smoke

Former British Vice-Consul in the Algarve, Donald Armstrong, told Peter Underwood, president of the Ghost Club, of the strange goings on at his childhood home in Newnham-on-Severn, which the 'ghost hunter' retold in his book *Ghostly Encounters.*

In the early 1950s, Donald Armstrong was lying in bed when he felt a heavy weight land on his feet. At first he thought it was the family's dog, but she wasn't even in the room.

Telling his mother about it the next morning, she told him that recently she had felt a sharp tapping on her shins for no reason. On another occasion, his father heard running steps up the main staircase and past his bedroom.

An aunt saw a woman in a crinoline gown going down the staircase into the first floor music room. She had seemed, she said, to be made up of 'rolling smoke'.

A Ghostly Lesson

Long Compton, near the famous Rollright Stones (themselves a favourite spot for ghosts), is only a mile outside of the Gloucestershire border. It is included here, though, not for any geographical reason but because it is associated with a fascinating story told in the chronicles of the Yorkshire abbey of Jervaulx, around the time of Edward III's reign.

According to the chronicles, St Augustine stopped at Long

Compton where the priest complained to him that the Lord of the manor had refused to pay tithe of his possessions to the church. The priest had threatened him with excommunication, but this had made no difference to the awkward lord.

Augustine called the lord of the manor to the church and discovered that he was every bit as stubborn as the priest had said. As he moved up to the altar to perform the Mass, Augustine cried out in a loud voice 'Let all those who are excommunicated leave the church'.

The lord left, but as he reached the churchyard a gravestone lifted up in front of him out of which drifted a ghost. It started to move across the churchyard until Augustine cried out from the church door for it to stop and tell its tale.

The ghost said he had been a Briton excommunicated when he had refused to pay tithes to the priest installed in his parish by the conquering Saxons. Augustine told him to point out the grave of the priest, whose ghost he also raised and ordered to absolve the Briton. Both ghosts were then sent back to their graves to rest in peace.

Not surprising, from that day the terrified lord of the manor never failed to pay his tithes.

By Royal Appointment

There has been a lot of talk by the media in recent years about Royal Gloucestershire, prompted by Prince Charles, Princess Anne and Prince and Princess Michael having homes in the county.

Never mentioned in these reports, though, is that a number of former kings and queens are evidently still living in Gloucestershire – well, their ghosts anyway.

Charles I, for instance, is said to haunt Court House in Painswick, where he was based when he ordered the Siege of Gloucester in 1643. Ghostly Cavaliers have also been seen in the gardens and grounds, presumably preparing themselves for the battle.

A few months after his execution, the headless ghost of the king appeared at Chavenage House near Tetbury, the home of Nathaniel Stephens, one of the county's two members in the House of Commons.

When Parliament went in to recess for Christmas 1648, Parliament was still split on whether the king should be executed or imprisoned. Stephens came home to Chavenage still uncertain of which was the right decision and over the Christmas break was visited by an uninvited guest, a Cromwellian officer named Colonel Ireton. After much discussion, Ireton managed to persuade Stephens to vote for regecide.

Charles I was beheaded on January 30th, 1649. Four months later, on May 2nd, Stephens fell ill and died, but not before he had expressed his regret for having agreed to the death of his king.

On the day of his funeral at Chavenage, the mourners were assembled in the courtyard ready to go in procession to the small church nearby when there was the sound of galloping horses. Into the courtyard came a splendid coach drawn by black horses. One can only imagine the horror of the mourners when they saw that it was driven by a headless man dressed in royal robes with the Garter on his leg and the star of that order on his breast. It was the ghost of Charles I.

The scene was to become even more terrifying. The main door of Chavenage House opened and the ghost of Nathaniel Stephens in his shroud stepped out and climbed into the coach.

The royal coachman whipped up the horses and moved off; as it reached the outer gate, the coach, horse, driver and passenger disappeared in flames.

Chavenage is also haunted by a grey lady. On April 13th, 1973, the *Wilts and Gloucestershire Standard* reported that she had been seen by Princess Marie Louise when she visited the mansion. Afterwards she always crossed herself when she entered or left the house.

Henry VIII and Anne Boleyn have been sighted at nearby Sheepscombe. They often visited this part of Gloucester on hunting trips with Sir William Kingston. Ironically, it was Kingston who, as Governor of the Tower of London, later had the sad task of being in charge of Anne while she awaited execution.

Her ghost has been sighted on numerous occasions in Sheepscombe Woods, sometimes with a smiling Henry. Both have been seen dressed as if for hunting, perhaps re-living happier days?

The last of Henry's six wives, Catherine Parr, was buried in the magnificent castle at Sudeley. But it is not a royal person who haunts the castle but the favourite hunting dog of Prince Rupert, who had made Sudeley his headquarters during the Civil War.

22

While the rest of Gloucestershire mostly sided with Parliament, Sudeley under George Brydges, sixth Lord Chandos, supported the Crown. Three times Sudeley came under siege before it finally fell in 1644. Prince Rupert's dog was a casualty of the first siege and its ghost was first sighted in 1643.

It is said that when it makes an appearance, usually in the ruins of the banqueting hall, it is a sign that some misfortune is to happen to a member of the family who owns the castle.

Gloucestershire was the scene for the decisive battle of the War of the Roses at Tewkesbury in 1471. Margaret of Anjou, wife of Henry VI, had landed at Weymouth believing she only had to march to London and with her husband secure the throne. She did not know then that Edward IV had had such a major victory at Barnet in which the Earl of Warwick, 'the Kingmaker', had been slain.

With her troops, the queen marched up through the West Country to Gloucester where she had expected to cross the Severn and join up with the Welsh, but the people of the city would not let her pass.

Instead, she had to march on to Tewkesbury where on May 4th her weary and demoralised soldiers engaged Edward's army and were soundly defeated. Her son, Edward the Prince of Wales, was put to death on the battlefield and Margaret taken to London where she was imprisoned for five years then exiled to France. Henry VI was placed in the Tower, where he was murdered.

On the march to Tewkesbury, Margaret stayed at Owlpen Manor near Uley, and her restless spirit is still supposed to haunt the house.

During the last war, a group of young evacuees stayed at Owlpen. On their first night, they were tucked up into bed by a woman in a beautiful, old-fashioned red gown, pointed hat and veil – Margaret of Anjou perhaps comforting children escaping the horror of a war four centuries after that in which she lost everything?

Owlpen is also said to be haunted by a black monk who, according to legend, was walled up and starved to death by the owners after fleeing the sacking of Kingswood Abbey.

King's Head, Cirencester

The King's Head in Market Place, Cirencester, has been haunted by a whole pack of ghosts in its long history, some charming (one invisible ghost with a strong perfume was once described as being a 'fairy') and at least one with malevolent tendencies.

Beneath the King's Arms, and in recent years used as a skittle alley, is a long cellar known as The Monks' Retreat. A block passage leads from here under the Market Place to the cellars of the Abbey Penitentiary. So it is only to be expected that a monk haunts this and other parts of the hotel.

There is also a more spirited spirit, seldom seen, who shakes curtains, moves objects about and open and shuts doors. He has also been known to hold hotel guests down in their beds but, thankfully for Cirencester's tourist trade, only on very rare occasions.

A fireball once 'danced' across the ballroom, though it has usually been explained as 'static electricity', which seems even more difficult to believe than that it was one of a whole catalogue of poltergeist activity experienced in the King's Head.

The most interesting ghost from an historical viewpoint is the ghost of a cavalier who pointed and fired a pistol at one of the hotel porters. It has been suggested that this event has nothing to do with the fact that Cirencester was a Royalist garrison town during the Civil War but that it is related to an incident that took place here in 1688, almost 40 years after that war had come to an end.

In 1688, Lord Lovelace had stopped in Cirencester on his way to join William of Orange prior to the bloodless, so-called Glorious Revolution which saw James II removed from the throne and replaced by William and Mary. A group of Stuart supporters, led by Captain Lorange, attacked Lovelace in the Market Place and shot one of his companions, Bulstrode Whitelock. The wounded man was taken to the King's Head, where he died.

Local legend has it that the cavalier ghost is Whitelock, still fighting to protect Lord Lovelace from his attackers outside the King's Head.

Trotter's Daughter

In the last century, The Coombs in the Forest of Dean town of Coleford was owned by chemical works owner, Isaiah Trotter.

According to Sue Law, a female member of the Trotter family fell in love with a stableboy and became pregnant by him. Knowing there was no future for her in the relationship and that she was unlikely to get much support from her family, she reached such a state of despair that in the end she hanged herself from a beam in the stables.

We don't know when The Coombs started to be haunted but in the 1970s new houses were built on the grounds of the big house, and it was in one of these that a white figure began to be seen. That the house was built close to the site of the old stables leads one to assume that it is the ghost of the poor Trotter girl.

The main house in which the Trotter family lived is now a residential home for the elderly and it too has been subjected to things that go bump in the night. Both residents and staff have heard screams, strange noises and talking in empty rooms. On one occasion a woman in grey was seen, though who she was no one knows.

There have also been numerous incidents of practical jokes and one poor visitor had the terrifying experience of seeing a barrage of snowballs materialise out of thin air and hurtle towards her.

In 1974 a large tree in what had been the garden of the big house was felled and as there were no further incidents it was thought that this had in some way stopped the haunting of The Coombs. But this doesn't seem to be the case, Sue Law stating that the ghost of The Coombs is still there, though she haunts the house less frequently these days.

Monks And Nuns

Some country people used to say that ghosts were souls of people too good for Hell but not good enough for Heaven, which begs the question – why is it that so many ghosts in Gloucestershire are of religious men?

Perhaps it is just a case of percentages? After all, the county has a huge number of very large churches, abbeys, monasteries and convents – leading to the often quoted phrase '. . . as sure as God's in Gloucestershire'.

In Gloucester itself are the remains of the centuries old Dominican priory of Blackfriars where, in daylight in 1870, Alice Godfrey saw a monk in prayer. She said that he had fixed staring eyes and a grey lined face.

During restoration work in 1969, a skull of a man, presumably a friar who had died from a head wound, was unearthed in the church nave.

According to a story in the *Gloucester Citizen* in January of that year, workman Gary Lane was working on a beam in the roof over the nave when he saw in front of him the ghost of a monk. Many of his colleagues saw the outline of a man in prayer and one saw a friar with blood pouring from his head running from the nave. What could have occurred here?

Nearby is Greyfriars, also formerly a priory. This is haunted, but not so much as the Greyfriars Inn. Here, furniture has been moved, loud noises have been heard, doors opened and lights switched on and off.

The *Gloucester Citizen* (November 15th, 1988) told how 39 year old builder Geoffrey Lovatt from Oxford, who was carrying out refurbishing work in the pub, was so scared by the ghostly activities that he fled and took refuge for the night – in a graveyard!

'I thought the dead would be a better bet than whatever was about at the Greyfriars Inn,' he told the *Citizen*.

The cathedral ought to be haunted by the ghost of Edward II, so horribly murdered at Berkeley and buried in the cathedral. But legend tells of a haunting by the spirit of a far less august person.

There's a story that when the cathedral was being built, a 14 year old apprentice fell from the scaffolding and died. So active was his ghost that eventually it was exorcised in the old way of tricking it into a bottle, which was sealed and buried in the foundations of one of the huge columns that support the roof of this great building. Where, presumably, it still lies.

Tewkesbury has a church that is as magnificent as many cathedrals. There was an Abbey here in Saxon times and an abbey

27

church was later built. The church, with its massive Norman tower and colossal west front arch, is haunted by a monk who leaves through the west door and walks in the direction of the vicarage.

Another in a black habit has been seen walking inside the abbey who then climbs up an invisible staircase before vanishing – he is obviously still 'living' in his old time.

A white lady has also been seen in the churchyard.

An inn with a very quaint name, the Old Corner Cupboard, now occupies the site of a monastery in Gloucester Street, Winchcombe. Perhaps it is the beer that persuaded the monks to stay on here? Others have been seen near the old railway station and at Pyke Bank.

Similarly, part of the Snowshill Arms in Snowshill was formerly a hostel for clergy visiting the priory here, and one hooded monk has remained.

Three monks were seen in the middle of Driffield Road, Lydney, another haunts the churchyard at Leonard Stanley near Stroud.

There is a blocked passage in the King's Head, Cirencester, which leads under the Market Place to the Abbey Penitentiary and a monk has been seen in the old inn.

What about much haunted Prestbury and Littledean? Yes, they have their monks too.

At Littledean Hall, a monk in white has been seen in what was once the library. While in Prestbury, an abbot in black habit walks from the church, through the churchyard to the 16th century Reform Cottage in Deep Street, whose garden is on the priory burial ground – but only at Easter, Christmas and All Saints' Day.

A less savoury monk, described by witnesses as 'leering', has also been seen in the town.

Charfield's Railway Children

Charfield is one of the villages that Gloucestershire lost during the local government re-organisation of the 1970s which led to the founding of the much disliked county of Avon.

It is returned to Gloucestershire here, though, because its haunting happened before the bureaucrats decided to muck-around with centuries-old boundaries. And because it is a poignant, mysterious and intriguing story.

Before dawn on the morning of October 13th, 1928, the normally quiet village was rocked by a devastating rail accident. The night express to Bristol ploughed into a slow-moving shunting engine crossing the main line. Then, to add to the horror, a third train, following the express, smashed into the wreckage.

Rescue workers were faced with a scene of unimaginable carnage. As they brought out the injured, the dying and the already dead, they discovered the remains of two children, a girl of about 7 and a boy of around 11.

Their identity was never discovered, their bodies never claimed.

The bodies of the two unwanted children were buried in Charfield churchyard under a grey granite memorial erected by the London, Midland and Scottish Railway. It contains the names of those who died and the rather pathetic line 'Two Unknown'.

And there have been occasional reports since then of the ghosts of Charfield's railway children having been seen wandering hand in hand near the site of that terrible rail crash.

Ram Inn, Wotton-under-Edge

The 17th century Ram Inn at Wotton-under-Edge is nowadays a private house but it is what one imagines a haunted pub should look like. Outside it has a black and white timbered gable, whitewashed walls and Cotswold tiles. Inside it is all exposed timbers and stonework.

But so active are its ghosts – at least five – that one group of visitors staying in the house became so scared that they left in the middle of the night by climbing through a window.

A cavalier, a lady called Elizabeth, Tom the Tramp, one or two monks and a shepherd have all been seen here.

Visitors have felt a strong presence in the building, heard bangings and strange noises, a bed was raised off the floor and the person sleeping in it thrown out.

In 1984, owner John Humphries told the *Bristol Evening Post* (Monday November 26th) that things had strangely got worse after someone sent him a copy of the will of previous owner, tanner Thomas Waight, dated 1694. When he received a photograph of another former landlord, Rufus Morley, the spirits became even more agitated.

Undoubtedly a major reason for all the activity was, he thought, because he had altered the inn during restoration work.

Mr Humphries said that he kept seeing the ghost of an old man which he thought might be Waight.

A local dowser told him that the 360 year old inn was built on a graveyard and that scores of bodies, some of them children killed in ancient religious rites, were buried there. One body, he said, was of a woman murdered by soldiers. When Mr Humphries dug up part of the floor he did indeed find the bones of a child.

It is one room in particular that has a terrible air of doom and despondency. He calls it the Bishop's Room.

'The presence is so very strong and awful that it will follow you out of the room, into the car park and along the road', Mr Humphries told Post reporter Allan Guy. 'Two men who stayed in the Bishop's Room had such a terrible experience they had to go to the church to be exorcised by the vicar. He banned them from entering the building again.'

Only The Money Was There

A man riding to Stroud where he was staying the night with friends, got completely lost in the snow in the hills above Dursley.

It got darker and darker as he desperately looked for shelter for himself and his horse. In the distance he saw a light. As he rode close to it, he saw to his relief that it was an inn; the Cotswold hills are no place to be lost on a snowy night.

The landlord was waiting to welcome him and a groom was on hand to lead his horse off to the stables. A servant showed the man up to a large bedroom where a very welcomed fire was roaring in the hearth. He was brought warm dry clothes and a huge meal, then he climbed into bed and fell asleep.

Next morning, his own clothes, cleaned and dried, had been laid out for him, so he dressed and went down for breakfast. Although his breakfast had been laid out for him, he didn't see either the landlord or any of his staff.

He looked around but all he could find was his horse, looking fit and well fed. Not knowing what to do, he left two guineas as payment on the table and continued his journey to Stroud.

On the way he met his friends, who had been worried when he had not arrived the night before and set out early that morning to find him. When he told them that he had stayed at an inn above Dursley they were puzzled. For there was no inn there.

Because he was so insistent, they let him show them the inn. When they got to the place, there was, of course, no inn, no landlord and no stables – but there, in the snow, were two gold guineas.

A similar sort of story comes from Cold Ashton near Bath.

In the 1930s, portrait painter Olive Snell was invited to stay for a weekend at the home of Lady Winifred Pennoyer in Charterhouse.

The painter got lost in the dark and in Cold Ashton, to the north of Bath, she stopped at a big house to ask directions. The wrought iron gates were not locked so she drove up to the house, an Elizabethan manor, and knocked on the door.

Her knocking was answered by a man who gave her full instructions on how to get to Charterhouse. Assuming him to be the butler, she tipped him half-a-crown and continued her journey.

Lady Pennoyer was puzzled by the story, for she knew Cold Ashton well and the only house she could think of that answered the description was empty and boarded up.

The next day they decided to drive over to Cold Ashton, where Olive Snell recognised the manor as the one she had visited the night before, but it was indeed all locked and boarded up.

Borrowing the key from the gardener, they opened the big wrought iron gates and went up to the house. On the doorstep was her half-a-crown.

Lady Pennoyer was associated with another interesting ghostly encounter. With two friends she visited Corsham in Wiltshire and in the churchyard they had a terrifying experience. In front of them appeared a tiny bad-tempered man, only about 2 ft 6 inches high. He is believed to be the form of an evil monk who once lived in Corsham.

The Nether Lypiatt Blacksmith

The main entrance to Nether Lypiatt, the Gloucestershire home of Prince and Princess Michael of Kent at Thrupp near Stroud is through a pair of extremely decorative wrought iron gates.

To most visitors they seem to be a perfect example of the metalworker's craft, but they were not perfect enough to save their maker's life.

The gates were made in 1704, when Nether Lypiatt was owned by Judge Charles Coxe, whose circuit was in Wales. Their maker was a blacksmith convicted of murder, or sheep-stealing according to some stories.

The blacksmith had been sentenced to be hanged, but Coxe made him an offer he could hardly refuse. If he could make a perfect pair of gates for Nether Lypiatt, the judge would repeal his sentence.

So, the blacksmith set to work, labouring night and day for two weeks producing a pair of ornate gates of exceptional quality. Indeed, the workmanship is so good that one must wonder if this really is the work of a local blacksmith, even one working in the knowledge tht his life depended on his skills.

The mean old judge though was not going to be satisfied and after a close inspection of every inch of the gates he found a tiny flaw and refused the craftsman his reprieve.

On January 25th the blacksmith was hanged and at midnight on this date the gates of Nether Lypiatt have been known to fly open and the ghost of their ill-served maker appears riding a white horse.

Was it coincidence that a short while after the blacksmith was hanged, the body of Judge Coxe was discovered in nearby Toadsmoor Woods? Or was this the blacksmith exacting his revenge from 'the other side'?

The present Royal residents have never to my knowledge publicly stated whether they have seen the ghostly gate-maker but previous owners certainly did.

When one couple, Simon and Suna Boyle, attempted to have the house exorcised it made the national newspapers (*The Daily Express*, January 28th, 1984). It wasn't only the ghost of the blacksmith that seems to have troubled the Boyles but also a man in a frock coat who was seen seated at the dining table, a lady in white in the garden and a grey lady with a shawl over her head. The latter was seen by a builder working in the attic but when he told the police that he had seen an intruder, the local policeman just replied that he had merely seen the local ghost.

Chariot Of Fire

Burford is just outside the county border but worthy of inclusion here because it can claim the most spectacular ghost ever supposed to have been seen in the region.

Lord Lawrence Tanfield, who bought the lordship of the manor in 1617 and became the first resident lord of the manor since the Norman Conquest, was distinctly unpopular in the Cotswolds. Not as much as his wife, though, who is alleged to have said that she would like to grind the Burford people to powder beneath her chariot wheels!

It was in a fiery chariot that Lady Tanfield's ghost is said to have ridden over the roofs of the town, sometimes accompanied by her husband. The sight of her, according to legend, is said to have foretold any misfortune likely to overtake Burford.

In the 18th century, a group of clergymen came together to exorcise her. They successfully managed to get her ghost into the church and into a bottle which they secured and threw into the Windrush underneath the first arch of the bridge.

Legend has it that if the river ever runs dry under the arch, Lady Tanfield would escape from the bottle and once more ride over the roofs of Burford in her fiery chariot. Which is a good enough reason for the people of Burford to keep a very watchful eye on the river whenever the water level starts to drop.

A Bomber's Target

During the last war, a German pilot returning from the bombing raid which devastated Coventry, dropped his remaining bombs on the A40 road between Salperton and Compton Abdale. Why he should have bombed an empty stretch of road is something of a mystery, but locals do have one explanation.

A ghostly horse and trap has regularly been seen near Hangman's Stone, at the crossroads on this part of the road. Often it bore lights. The suggestion is that the pilot saw these lights and thought he was over a town otherwise covered by black-out.

Woodchester's Secrets

Woodchester's principal treasure, its remarkable 48 sq ft Roman mosaic pavement, is kept preserved by a covering of soil and only rarely is it uncovered and its beauty revealed to the public.

This is not the only hidden treasure in this village near Stroud. Hidden away in a deeply wooded valley is an unfinished Gothic masterpiece Woodchester Park.

The house, designed by the young Victorian architect Benjamin Bucknall for wealthy Liverpool merchant William Leigh, was begun in 1854. To build it, Leigh demolished a house, Spring Park, which had belonged to Earl Ducie.

Work on Woodchester Park continued for 14 years, and then stopped, probably because of financial problems. It has remained unfinished and relatively unknown outside of the area ever since.

Today it is maintained by a Trust who rent it from the local district council for a peppercorn rent.

A number of ghosts are said to haunt Woodchester Park and were investigated by the Geoff Bird of the Associations for the Scientific Study of Anomalous Phenomena (ASSAP).

These included a headless centurion, a ragged dwarf and a coffin that hovers over one of the estate's lakes, possibly a Dominican friar who committed suicide by drowning.

There's a black dog whose appearance was thought to herald the imminent death of a Dominican.

And most unusual, the ghosts of two American servicemen have been seen in the park, presumably something to do with the fact that US troops were stationed in Woodchester during the last war.

The present warden, William Billett has been reported as having experienced no ghostly goings-on:

'I don't believe all these ghost stories and I can honestly say I have not experienced anything at all,' he told the *Western Daily Press* newspaper (January 29th, 1993.)

'It is a very nice place and very secluded . . . of course it is very quiet at night, as you would expect it to be, but I don't mind a bit.'

Littledean Hall

Littledean Hall, or Dean Hall as it is also known locally, in the Forest of Dean claims to be England's oldest house and one of its most haunted.

The house goes back to the 10th or 11th centuries, the cellar below the north front being the remains of a Saxon hall. The present Jacobean Hall was built in 1612. A Roman temple was discovered in the grounds, thought to have been a water shrine to Sabrina, Goddess of the Severn. It is perhaps to this shrine that the platoon of Roman soldiers, seen in Silver Street in Littledean are still marching after all these centuries?

Littledean also boasts an 11th or early 12th century earthworks called The Old Castle of Dean and a 14th century church containing a Saxon arch.

The Pyrke family owned the Hall for two and a half centuries and in 1744 a young black servant murdered 23-year old Charles Pyrke after discovering that he had fathered a child as a result of a liaison with his sister.

The young black servant, wearing a silver collar, has been seen on numerous occasions since then, on the landing outside his garret bedroom at the top of the East Wing, with a lighted candle outside the drawing room and on at least one occasion in daylight hours. He has also been blamed for constantly removing flowers from vases and throwing them on the floor.

A painting hung over the mantlepiece was found several times lying in the grate having 'fallen' off its hooks. The owners tried hanging it with a strong chain but this mysteriously broke. Eventually they gave up and left that wall unadorned, until 1982 when a reproduction of a painting of Pyrke and the servant, painted when they were young boys, was hung over the mantlepiece which has remained undisturbed.

A bloodstain on the floorboards in the dining room has stubbornly refused to go away, despite scrubbing and even planing. It just kept on coming back.

In the spring of 1644, Roundhead soldiers attacked the Hall and captured 20 soldiers in the guardshouse. Inside the house were a few private soldiers and Colonel Congreve, governor of Newnham, and Captain Wigmore who was in charge of the garrison. They gave themselves up, but one of their soldiers fired and killed a Parliament trooper.

In the skirmish that followed, the Royalists were all killed, including Congreve and Wigmore who died inside the house. It is their blood, so it is said, that stains the dining room floor.

The dining room is also haunted by a monk who walks from here to the library where there was a priest's hole leading to a tunnel from the cellar to the Grange of Flaxley Abbey, a quarter of a mile away. The tunnel would have been used by a monk from the Abbey when he secretly visited the house to give Holy Communion. People exploring the ruins of the Grange have been scared by noises, shadows and shapes, not to mention a strange and frightening white mist.

The Blue Bedroom at Littledean Hall is so haunted that for many years no one slept in it. Earlier occupants said it had a terrible atmosphere and they heard the sound of clashing swords, which ties in with a story that two brothers fought over a lady at Littledean and both were killed in the duel.

The ghost of a member of the Brayne family, who occupied the house for around 200 years (Richard Brayne who lived here in the middle of the 16th century was High Sheriff of Gloucester) is said to haunt the drive in the form of a ghostly gardener who sweeps up leaves – legend has it that during the Civil War one of the Braynes disguised himself as a gardener when hiding from the Roundheads. There are also stories of a lady in yellow having been seen around the house.

It is not only in the Hall that strange figures have been seen. According to a local story there was one house in the village that was so haunted that nobody would stay in it. It became so bad that in the end villagers wouldn't even go near it. After a succession of tenants, the house, whose location is unknown, remained empty for so long that it deteriorated to the point where it had to be pulled down.

The reason for this activity, says the legend, is that a suicide pact took place there between a brother and sister who had been living incestuously and had given birth to a baby girl. They couldn't stand being ostracised by everyone, he had lost his job and eventually they killed themselves and the baby.

The Red House, at the bottom of Littledean Hill, which dates back to soon after the Norman invasion, was once used as a Friends

Littledean Hall – claimed to be England's oldest, and one of its most haunted, houses.

Meeting House, so the ghostly man in his tall black hat seen walking through the gate could have been a Quaker.

Elsewhere in the village, a man in a velvet cap and cape has been seen at the Littledean House Hotel; a lady in grey at the 17th century Church Farm and the 13th century former inn The Old Vic, was said to be haunted.

Weird noises, shadows and shapes have been heard in the ruins of Littledean Grange as well as a 'frightening' white mist. Sue Law in her book on *Ghosts of the Forest of Dean* includes an anonymous dialect poem about a ghost rider and horse seen at the Grange.

The old Littledean Jail was bought and converted into offices by the Gloucester based Ecclesiastical Insurance Company in July 1988. One night a security man found a door had opened by itself, a six inch key had been turned in its lock and iron bolts undone. Staff working here at night have heard the sound of people walking about upstairs when no one else was in the building. Research hasn't found any incidents in the jail's history that could have caused such activity.

At Guns Mills, so-called not because firearms were made here but because it was owned by a man called Gun in the 17th century, a bent figure carrying a sack on its back has been seen, perhaps one of the monks that haunt the area around St Anthony's Well, which, because of its curative properties, was once a place of pilgrimage.

Snowshill Manor

National Trust administered Snowshill Manor, built in the 16th century on the site of the manor given by Kenulf, King of Mercia, to the Abbey of Winchcombe, is best known to visitors for the fascinating collection of objets d'art it contains.

Former owner Charles Wade, an avid collector since a boy, bought Snowshill Manor after the First World War and restored it specifically to contain and display his collections.

When he gave Snowshill Manor to the National Trust in 1951, it was packed with a weird assortment of toys, mechanical objects, clocks, locks, domestic bygones, Japanese Samurai armour, bicycles, witchcraft paraphenalia and much more.

It is, however, a previous owner who interests us here.

Charles Marshall lived at Snowshill during the last century and after death seems to have never left the house.

Farm labourer Richard Carter encountered the ghost of Charles Marshall, riding on a black pony, on a number of occasions and eventually challenged it. The spectre told him to meet him later that night in one of the farm buildings.

Carter went to the barn as instructed. At midnight the ghost appeared and gave him a secret message to pass on to Mrs Marshall.

According to local legend, this message contained details of a stash of money that Marshall had hidden in the house which, it is conjectured, is how Mrs Marshall could suddenly afford to begin erecting new buildings on the Snowshill estate.

During renovations, Charles Wade, who died in 1956, sent a small piece of timber from the house to a clairvoyant in Sussex.

Despite not being given any clue as to the identity of the building from which it came, the clairvoyant was able to describe the house and told him that in a room in an upper floor she saw a girl in a 17th century style green dress who didn't live there and would not stay the night.

After much research, Wade discovered a fascinating piece of history that corroborated the clairvoyant's story.

On St Valentine's day, 1604, a 16-year old heiress named Anne Parsons was secretly married against her will in Snowshill Manor. Her groom, Anthony Palmer, was after her fortune.

As the clairvoyant had said, poor Anne Parsons refused to spend her wedding night in the house, forcing the wedding party to make an uncomfortable midnight journey from Snowshill to Chipping Campden.

The local vicar of Snowshill, a Mr Stone, performed the ceremony and for his part in the affair was eventually brought before the Star Chamber.

Hair of the Dog

The Bowl Inn in Lower Almondsbury (now Avon) may be unique amongst British haunted pubs, for its ghost is a young French child who died in the village in 1708.

The girl has been heard crying and was seen in the late 1970s by the landlord's daughter, who also heard her reciting nursery rhymes.

A plaque inside the local church tells us more about the girl, Elizabeth Maronne and her brother John. The plaque reads:

Their father, a poor man, born in the parish of Dophin in the kingdom of France, believes that his sins were the cause that God took the life of his children.

Local people believe that the girl was badly treated by her father and so has returned to haunt the village.

The Bowl Inn is also said to have been haunted by two women whose identity is not known.

Pubs are frequently the setting for ghost tales, perhaps because in many villages they are the oldest surviving buildings. At the Hambrook Inn in Hambrook, also now in Avon, a friendly ghost called Ollie caused a lot of mischief in the first half of the last decade. Landlord Les Breakwell told the *Western Daily Press* in 1984 (March 15th) that Ollie began his tricks soon after he and his wife Joyce and their grown-up son Darren moved into the pub in 1982.

'The first strange thing was when our dog acted oddly when he went into the lounge. He would stir, his hair would go up and after a while he would bark at something in a corner. But there was nothing there. After a bit he would wag his tail. So we knew it was nothing really bad.'

Ollie would turn the coffee machine on, switch on lights, move glasses along the bar, roll barrels around the cellar and cause other mischief.

'I would go down to the cellar to put on the real ale and find it was already on. Then I would go back to take it off and it was off. The glass washer turned on of its own accord. Even the beer started flowing one night without the tap being turned on.'

41

Radar Or Martyrs?

In 1974 David Price and his wife Ruby built their own bungalow in Oakle Street, near Churcham.

They were then troubled by a long series of terrifying incidents. As many as 40 fires broke out and 30 burst water pipes. Light bulbs exploded and windows shattered, five puppies died in strange circumstances.

The Fire Brigade, electricity and water officials and environmental health officers investigated and were stumped by the phenomena; Nottingham University experts thought that radar might be the cause, linked with the Malvern radar base and GCHQ spy centre at Cheltenham.

In 1991, a London based psychic healer visited the bungalow and told the owners that a mound in their garden hid the burial place of monks and nuns who were burned to death in the 10th century.

Troubled Trouble House

The Trouble House Inn, on the A433 Tetbury to Cirencester road, is aptly named, for it has long been troubled by a ghost of a girl in her early 20s dressed in a dark blue dress. She has been seen in various parts of the building, but most especially in one of the bedrooms. The last sighting was in 1992.

Landlady Mrs Pat Robins tells an interesting story. When the tale of the Trouble House Inn ghost appeared in a newspaper in 1990, an 80 year old lady made the journey from Bristol to the inn to talk to Mrs Robins.

It seemed that she had lived there when she was a child and that her father used to beat her for saying she had seen the lady. After all these years, she had at last been proven right and had wanted to thank Mrs Robins.

Jack Hallam's *The Haunted Inns* tells of chain dragging noises at The Trouble House and a heavy wooden door unbarring itself and swinging open, but Mrs Robins says that in the 20 years they have been tenants her family have only ever seen the blue lady. And that the ghost was also seen by the previous landlord.

It is not surprising that the inn is troubled, considering its history. During the Civil War, a group of Royalists drinking in what was then called The Wagon and Horses were surprised by a band of Parliamentarians and a number were killed in the skirmish.

Two highwaymen, Mathias and Henry Finnel, were captured at the inn in 1829 and ended their days at the end of a rope.

In the 1830s, rioting farm labourers protesting against the introduction of labour saving machinery fought with soldiers here and a number of men and women were arrested.

When the inn was being reconstructed around this time, the owner ran out of money half way through the work and hanged himself in the pub. The next owner also had financial difficulties and ended up drowning himself in a nearby pond.

But the identity of the girl who haunts the inn is not known, nor why she should still trouble the Trouble House.

Mill Inn, Withington

According to local stories, an elderly woman drowned in the river by the Mill Inn at Withington, near Cheltenham. Perhaps it was her that landlord David Foley saw in 1990.

'I thought I had accidently locked someone in the pub when I saw her sitting there in a chair by the fire,' he told a local journalist. 'But then I realised we had checked everywhere before locking up and decided to run for it.'

He got as far as the passageway to his flat before he looked behind him – there she was again, but this time there were the outlines of two men standing behind her.

He described her as being about four feet six inches tall and wearing a wide brimmed hat with a veil over her face.

'After I got through the door I slipped the bolts pretty quickly. I didn't get much sleeping done that night.'

Present landlord Philip Roystone has been at the Mill Inn for only a year. 'We haven't seen anything yet, but we're looking forward to it – we think!' he told me.

One of his staff, however, saw an old couple sitting in the window of the bar at closing time. When she asked them to leave they took no notice. She asked again, but still no response. It must have looked very peculiar to the other people in the bar who saw her talking to two empty seats.

Frocester's Bell

A little way outside of the village of Frocester, on the road to Coaley, are the remains of a church. Only the tower, a portion of the porch and the graveyard remains.

When it became redundant a group of bellringers decided to steal the bells one night. They found the tower unlocked, climbed up to the bell chamber and unhitched one of the smaller bells.

They carried it down the stairs and left it on a landing. When they returned in a few minutes a little old lady was sitting on the bell. They asked her to move but she took absolutely no notice. In the end they decided that as it was a lightweight bell and she couldn't weigh more than a feather, they would lift it and her down the rest of the stairs.

But they couldn't shift the bell. They pushed it, they pulled it, but still it would not move. And all the time, the little old lady sat on top of it, taking no notice of the men or what they were doing.

It was then that they realised that something was very peculiar about this old lady and made a very hasty exit.

In the morning, the bell was found still halfway down the stairs but there was no sign of the old lady.

According to local stories, a Frocester woman had given the bell to the church and that she threw some of her jewellery into the molten metal as it was being cast.

Perhaps it was her at the tower that night, preventing her bell from being taken from the church?

The church at Frocester.

Over The Water

Ghostly encounters usually happen when people are on their own or occasionally with one other person. Collective sightings are pretty rare, which makes what happened on December 17th, 1937, particularly interesting.

On this evening, 18 members of the Easter Compton Prize Band had gone to sing carols at Over Court, an Elizabethan Manor near Almondsbury – now in Avon and not to be confused with the Over Court in Bisley.

This was something the band had done regularly at Christmas and they were well aware of local stories about the house being haunted by a white lady, though probably none of them expected to actually see her.

Over 50 years later, in 1988, a member of the band, John Purnell, told writer John Hudson what he saw that night. Purnell, who was only 14 in 1937, says that they had finished singing and were walking back through the entrance arch when they saw the apparition.

'In the tangle of undergrowth, hedge and trees to the left, the full moon was throwing odd shadows – but it could not obscure the fact that there was a bright white figure.'

It was seen floating just above the ground and a bluish glow radiated from it.

'It was about the size of an average person with a tall pointed head-dress, and it moved in a zig-zag manner away from us. It appeared to go behind trees and through a hedge and became smaller as it moved away and eventually disappeared. I suppose the episode lasted about 30 seconds.'

According to legend, the wife of an owner of Over Court had had an affair with a young man from a local family. Her husband found out and shot her. She was severely wounded but managed to drag herself away from the house and down to the bottom of the garden where she drowned in the fish pond.

She died on December 17th, and it has always been on that date that her ghost has been seen to rise from the pond.

There is a strange footnote to this. Two brothers were said to have seen the ghost and some months later, one of them was found drowned in the same fish pond.

She is not the only ghost at Over Court. A local postman

delivering letters to the house early one morning saw a footman in a striped waistcoat sitting on a farm stile. The footman smiled at him then disappeared.

Nor is she the only Gloucestershire ghost to rise from the water. A woman carrying a baby emerged from Swan Pool near Newland in the Forest of Dean.

The most notable of this sort of case has been recorded at Kempsford. At the end of the 13th century, Kempsford was part of the dower of Maud, daughter of Sir Patrick Chaworth, and wife of Henry III's grandson, Henry Plantagenet, the third Earl of Lancaster.

Against Maud's advice, Henry joined the barons and Simon de Montfort in their fight with Henry III and when injured supporters of the King started making their way across the Thames at Kempsford she secretly gave them refuge in the castle. One of these was her own brother-in-law whom she hid and brought food.

Her secret was discovered and someone turned the mind of the Earl against his wife, implying that she was having an affair with his brother. The Earl was so angry he hit his brother and then threw his innocent wife over the walls into the Thames below. And her ghost, walking on the surface of the water, haunts Kempsford to this day.

As for the Earl, her husband, he was so saddened by what he had done that he returned to the fighting and eventually died on the battlefield.

Far more terrifying must be the sight that has been seen at Soudley Ponds in the Dean, where a terror-stricken white horse appears, snorting and neighing as it struggles in vain to climb out of the water.

The story behind this would be quite comical if it hadn't ended so tragically. Around the middle of the last century, a farmer from Westbury on Severn by the name of William Bartlett regularly made the journey to Coleford and back, usually stopping on the return journey at most of the inns on the way.

By the time he had got to Soudley he was often so drunk that his friends would tie him on his horse knowing that it would find its own way home. But on the last occasion, the horse and its drunken rider didn't make it home. A terrible storm made the Forest paths treacherous, the horse slipped and they both drowned in the ponds.

Down In The Mine

When hammering noises started coming from the bottom of the pit shaft of the Pantod Mine at the top of Ruardean Hill, it took three searches before a body was found.

Strangely, it was the body of a man who had been dead long before the noises were heard!

Two different stories exist to explain the haunting of this pit. One is that the ghost was that of a mean mine owner who employed a small workforce of only six or so colliers to work the Pantod Mine. According to local legend, when he refused to pay his men their full wages there was a quarrel at the top of the mine which ended with the owner crashing down the pit shaft.

Whether he fell accidently or was pushed has never been resolved, though one can make a shrewd guess by the fact that, so the story goes, none of his colliers bothered to make any effort to get him out or even to raise the alarm!

There is, however, a near-contemporary autobiography by Timothy Mountjoy (*The Life, Labours and Deliverances of a Forest of Dean Collier*, 1887) which tells a slightly different story.

According to Mountjoy, the man was a stone mason nicknamed Get-it-to-go who disappeared around 1840 after a drunken argument and brawl in a local inn.

Twelve months later, stories began to circulate of noises coming from down the old pit and rumours soon linked them with the disappearance of the stone mason.

The local constables made a search of the bottom of the old shaft and could find nothing unusual, but the hammering noises increased and so, 18 months later, an equally unsuccessful search was carried out.

On searching the mine a third time, though, the constables discovered an unidentified body, presumed to be that of the missing man, which was placed in a coffin and brought to the surface where a huge crowd had gathered.

Like any group of people who work in dangerous occupations, miners tend to be a superstitious lot, and considering the number of stories of haunted pits and mines, they probably have good reason.

The Forest of Dean, riddled with workings, has many interesting stories to tell.

There's an unusual story, for instance, associated with the Speedwell Pit. In the 1830s, Phillip Symonds, a 21-year old collier from St Briavels, died after being suffocated by gas while working in this pit. After that, colliers reported that they were being warned of gas by a strange coughing in the tunnels.

Miners in Clearwell Caves, an ancient iron mine now open to the public, used to tell of an old man in 14th century mining clothes who haunted the tunnels.

The Ham Mine nearby is also haunted by a miner and Sue Law in her book *Ghosts of the Forest of Dean* tells how a group of workers from the Rank Xerox photocopier factory in Mitcheldean foolishly decided to go ghost hunting in the mine.

They had heard about a television crew filming in Ham who had fled after seeing the ghost of a miner. They were no braver, however, and left with similar speed when they encountered a ghostly man with a pick axe in one hand and a candle on a stick in the other!

The ghost of a miner killed by a truck on the tram line which crosses what is now the back of a car park near Clearwell has an unusual style of his own. One man parked his car on the lines and when he got home discovered in the light that his clothes were covered in black bootmarks – worse, when he went back to the car he found a line of footprints on the roof inside his car!

Dashing Away With A Ghostly Iron

Most people would dread the thought of sharing their home with a ghost or indeed any form of spirit. The Talbot Hotel in Tetbury, however, has the sort of ghost most people would welcome with open arms – an old lady who does the ironing!

In 1984, a chambermaid who had recently joined the staff noticed on several occasions an old lady with her hair drawn back in a bun, busy doing the ironing in one of the upstairs rooms.

When owner Audrey Speak remarked that she had a pile of ironing to do, the chambermaid asked why she didn't give it to the old lady to do.

On being questioned, the chambermaid, described by Ray Speak as a 'perfectly sensible, level-headed person', described the old lady she had seen in the upstairs rooms.

Audrey and Ray Speak, who had at this time been running The Talbot for two years, didn't employ any such person. They then realised they had a ghost on their hands.

The Talbot is no longer an inn but holiday accommodation, and though they were told about it by Mr and Mrs Speak when they bought the building in 1986, present owners George and Gill Twigg have never seen the ironing ghost.

Mrs Twigg does, however, raise an important point: the room in which the ghost was seen contains no fireplace and no chimney. So, how did she heat her iron unless she was a very modern ghost using electricity?

Although she has never seen this ghost, Mrs Twigg did have a ghostly encounter soon after they bought the Talbot. Standing outside a part of the building that was completely locked up, she saw a figure cross a window, which she assumed to be her husband until he appeared coming down the stairs behind her.

'It didn't particularly worry me,' she said. 'Maybe there is a presence here, but no one has experienced anything but a pleasant friendly atmosphere.'

Orchestral Manoeuvres In The Dark

In 1974 at St Mary's Church, Dodington, the tomb of Lady Georgiana Codrington, daughter of the seventh Duke of Beaufort, was opened up because rising damp had been discovered.

From that day on, ghostly piano playing was heard in nearby Dodington House, the Codrington family home. It was heard by members of the family, including Lady Georgiana's great grandson Major Simon Codrington, by the staff and by visitors. The piano lid was also found open on occasions.

One night, 80 members of the International Police Federation dined at the house and after their meal, the candles flickered and the piano playing was clearly heard by everyone at the table. It was, by all accounts, in the style of Chopin.

Lady Georgiana Codrington, who died in 1881, had been a gifted pianist.

And the family vault at St Mary's is connected to the cellars of Dodington House by a network of tunnels.

Another musical ghost haunts Sundial Cottage in Prestbury, but this time it is the spinet that is heard. There are two explanations, one that it is a music professor who used to live here, while other tales tell of a young girl having been seen playing the spinet.

The Garricks Head pub in Bath Street, Cheltenham, used to have an old, out of tune piano, but the one that the pub's ghost was playing was in perfect order.

In 1986, owner Ray Shepphard described the piano to a *Western Daily Press* reporter (November 7th): 'It's useless. It's damp, tuneless and rotten, but those who have heard the stirring music have said it was note perfect. The playing has been quite magnificent, and the people who heard it were not drunk either.'

It is not just piano playing that has been heard here, but also sea shanties and even orchestral pieces. A possible explanation is that the inn was built on the site of an old theatre.

The piano was restored and retuned, and the ghost seems to have disappeared. The present landlord, who came to the Garricks Head in 1987, states that he has had no experiences of any ghost in the pub.

I don't know of any accounts yet of a ghostly rock guitarist, though there is a refreshingly modern motorcyclist who haunts the road outside the police station in Coleford, Forest of Dean.

And, back in Prestbury, a singing ghost haunted a cottage in the High Street during the 1950s and early Sixties but then stopped – perhaps it felt it couldn't compete with The Beatles?

The Ragged Cot Inn at Hyde.

Ragged Cot, Hyde

Business must have been bad in 1760 for Bill Clavers, landlord of the Ragged Cot in the small Golden Valley village of Hyde, between Minchinhampton and Chalford.

Taking inspiration from the highwaymen who made travel so precarious in these times, Clavers decided to rob the night coach from London.

He needed a lot of Dutch courage though and was drinking heavily as he prepared himself for the night's escapade. When it was time, he grabbed his pistols and staggered out of the bedroom. His pregnant wife tried to stop him but he pushed her aside so violently that she fell down the stairs.

Clavers rode off and robbed the coach as planned, but when he arrived home, with the constables on his heels, he discovered a gruesome scene. There was his wife lying dead at the foot of the stairs and next to her the body of a newly born child.

In sheer panic, he stuffed their bodies into a large wooden trunk just as the constables arrived at the Ragged Cot. Clavers shot one of them, so the others stayed back to try and work out a plan.

Just as they were about to rush the inn they heard a terrible cry from Clavers – he had just seen the ghosts of his wife and child cross the hall and disappear up the stairs.

After that, the terrified Clavers was easily captured by the constables who searched the building and discovered the trunk's terrible contents, but not before one of them had seen a woman with a baby in her arms watching the proceedings.

St Briavels

High above the River Wye near Bigsweir stands St Briavels Castle, originally built seven hundred years ago as part of the Norman defences to protect this part of England from marauding Welsh armies.

Today, the castle is a youth hostel, well placed for exploring the beautiful Wye Valley and the Forest of Dean. Once though it was a prison, inhumane even by 17th century standards.

It only had one tiny window and prisoners slept two to a bed. Hangings were carried out inside the prison as well as outside and there was an oubliette, a concealed dungeon with a trap door in the ceiling as its only opening, from which a prisoner did not expect to emerge alive.

One prisoner left a piece of graffiti that has survived over 320 years: 'Rob Belcher, the day will come that thou shalt answer for it, for thou has sworn against me, 1671'.

T.A. Ryder recorded at least three ghosts in the castle: a man in armour, a lady in white and a man in very old fashioned costume.

During repair work in the main room, a wall in one corner was partially demolished uncovering a small chamber containing a skeleton, perhaps someone who had taken refuge there and been unable to escape.

One Youth Hosteller told Peter Underwood a particularly horrific story of the one night he stayed in St Briavels. He was woken by a noise from beneath his dormitory window that he gradually realised was the sound of people chanting. This was followed by a scream, cheering crowds and a particularly spine-chilling scream from a young girl that got louder and higher in pitch as if she was being subjected to more and more pain.

Only one other person in the hostel heard the same horrific screams.

In St Briavels village, a rather poignant story is associated with the ghost of a young girl at Cinderhill House.

The father of a young girl called Emmaline had arranged that she should marry an older man, despite the fact that she loved another. On her wedding day she ran out of the church in the middle of the service, down Cinderhill to the well into which she jumped and drowned.

The George Inn is also haunted and ghostly footsteps have been heard along the upstairs corridor.

Gazetteer Of The Ghosts Of Gloucestershire

Almondsbury

The Bowl Inn in Lower Almondsbury is haunted by an 18th century French girl, Elizabeth Maronne, who died and is buried in the parish churchyard.

Arlingham

Old lady seen inside the church in 1902, said to be Mrs Budge, vicarage housekeeper. Woman in her nightdress seen running across a field known as The Spurts (but interestingly originally known as The Spirits). On May 24th, 1757, a ghostly funeral was seen making its way up the drive of the Court House. A year later to the day saw the death of John Yate, the last male heir to the estate. Grey lady glides through the courtyard of Slowwe House, waits on the landing, stands in the bedroom watching the sleepers.

Aust

Screams of Parliament troops drowned in the Severn during the Civil War. Also noise of a pack of the Berkeley Hunt hounds that fell over the cliff into the river, perhaps chasing a ghostly fox?

Avening

Ghostly figure seen in the lane from Weighbridge Inn to Minchin-hampton, supposedly at the place where a member of the Playne family died in last century.

Berkeley

It was in Berkeley Castle that Edward II was terribly tortured to death with a red hot spit, his shrieks were heard not just in the castle but also in Berkeley itself. Considering the nature of his death, it is not surprising that some locals have heard his screams at night.

Birdlip

Four Neolithic warriors, carrying spears, seen at West Tump long barrow near Birdlip. A helpful ghost has given directions to lost travellers on Birdlip Hill.

Bishop's Cleeve

A man in Puritan style dress (black coat, whitecollar, knee breeches etc) seen at communion in village church. Stage coach, complete with passengers, seen emerging from a wall of the Farmer's Arms on the A435 Cheltenham to Evesham road.

Bisley

Headless horsemen riding past The Giant's Stone in Dead Man's Lane, the road between Bisley and Bibury. Group of headless men at Money Tump, a prehistoric round barrow to the south of the village.

Burford

Just outside the county border; ghost of Lady Tanfield rode over the roof-tops in a fiery chariot. Exorcised in the 18th century.

Cam

Local tradition had it that a ghost was imprisoned at Lower Knapp Farm beneath a stone at the top of the steps leading from the hallway to the cellar. He would not appear as long as grass didn't grow on the stone. According to local historian T.A. Ryder, occupants of the farm used to pour boiling water on to the stone to ensure that nothing grew on it.

Cambridge

Meredith in *The Haunted Cotswolds* tells of an unidentified house on the Bristol Road where an elderly man in a trilby hat and light coloured raincoat was regularly seen on Saturday nights, once with an alsatian dog, in one of the bedrooms. Sound of dice being thrown and music also heard downstairs. The family had lived in the house for 26 years without any sign of a ghost; as so often is the case, activity only started after alterations had been made.

Charfield

The ghost of two children, a boy and a girl, by railway track. Suggested it was the two children who died in the rail crash of 1928 – they were never identified nor were their bodies ever claimed, so they were buried in churchyard.

Cheltenham

On New Year's Eve, 1939, Margo Vincent Smith saw a nun at 6.15 pm in a girls' school – now a private residence – in Cheltenham. The head of the school and Miss Vincent Smith watched the nun sit down on an invisible chair in the playground. The nun was seen after that, always on New Year's Eve.

ARLE: Poltergeist activity, name calling, outline of a human shape on one of the beds, clocks and watches altered, name of a member of the occupying family written on paper in a typewriter in a cupboard etc.

BAYSHILL ROAD: Little girl who was drowned by the butler in a pool in the garden of a house in Bayshill Road, seen in the garden and in the bedrooms. A small old man also reported.

CHARLTON HOUSE, Cirencester Road: Well dressed man in top hat, cape and carrying silver topped cane and another in sporting tweeds.

COLLEGE: man in raincoat.

CORONATION SHOPPING CENTRE: Hester's Way. Disappearing female shopper.

GARRICKS HEAD, Bath Road: Piano player.

HATHERLEY ROAD: Lady in grey. Poltergeist activity.

HOSPITAL: Man in white shroud, nurse in old-fashioned uniform.

NAUNTON CRESCENT: Old woman in black appeared when a child was sick and not seen since her recovery.

NORTHFIELD TERRACE, Clarence Street: Small old lady.

OLD BATH ROAD: A ghost plays the piano in the Garricks Head pub. Wilf Cox, a noted ghost expert, and his family lived in a house in Old Bath Road. An old lady in dark clothes appeared in his garden and told him that she used to live in the house and had come back to look around. When he took his eyes off her, she disappeared. The house had, during the last war, been a home for elderly ladies evacuated from the South Coast. Also many reports of an old man searching for his dog in the streets of this area.

OLD CROWN HOTEL, High Street: Ghost of a young girl. There's a story that a child was killed here by being baked in the ovens when the old part of the inn was a bakery.

THE PARK: Woman on horse rides through a large house and up and down the stairs.

PITTVILLE CIRCUS ROAD: St Anne's, originally called Garden Reach. Tall lady in black regularly seen. Investigated by Society for Psychical Research.

PITTVILLE LAKE: Carriage and horses beneath the water; female figure rises from the lake.

SUFFOLK ARMS: Tapping noises in the cellar.

TEWKESBURY ROAD: A group of pikemen at the junction of Tewkesbury Road and Old Gloucester Road seen in early 1980s.

Cinderford

Ghost of a woman who founded a hermitage in the St White's area before the town was established, seen in White's Road.

SHAPRIDGE HILL: A most unusual manifestation has been sighted in a field near Abenhall church – not a person but a whole building, a mill that was demolished in the last century.

SPEEDWELL PIT: Coughing miner (Philip Symonds, died from gas suffocation in 1830s) gave warning of gas.

Cirencester

An old lady in grey, sighted on three known occasions in the Black Horse Hotel, Castle Street. She scratched a man's name in one of the bedroom window panes.

At the King's Head in Market Place, there have been reports of the sighting of a monk, doors opening, guests report being held down, footsteps, a 'fireball' dancing across the ballroom and a cavalier who fired an old flint lock pistol at a porter.

TAR BARROW HILL: According to the Bodleian Rawlinson papers, written by William Budden and printed in 1685, two men digging gravel at the foot of Tar Barrow Hill just outside Cirencester discovered the entrance to the barrow. Inside they found a number of rooms full of furniture, urns etc which crumbled to dust when touched. In one room they were startled to find themselves face to face with a man in armour, carrying what has been described as a truncheon and a light in a glass. As they approached, the man lunged at them three times, the third time smashing the light. The men made a hasty exit and as they left the barrow the roof caved in, burying everything.

Clearwell

Lady in red in Clearwell Castle. Old man in 14th century mining clothes haunted the tunnels of Clearwell Caves; a miner with a pick axe in one hand and a candle on a stick in the other in Ham Mine. Ghost of a miner killed by a truck on the tram line which crosses the back of a commercial car park 'walked' over a car parked across the tram line. A tall man wearing a trilby hat and carrying a shopping bag and walking stick seen in the middle of the road from Trow Green to Clearwell. In Puzzlewood, at ancient iron workings, imaginatively landscaped and open to the public, a ghostly, savage black dog seen snarling in the top of a cavern.

Cold Ashton

Ghost of a man opened door of the manor house in the 1930s and gave directions to painter Olive Snell who had lost her way.

Coleford

Man and boy seen, hand in hand, crossing the Cinderford to Coleford road, said to be ghosts of two people who were killed here by a horse and cart. The ghost of a cavalier knocks at the door of the old Angel Inn in the centre of the Forest of Dean town. Carriage and four people seen in Bream Road.

The Coombs was once a large estate. A white figure, thought to be the ghost of a girl who committed suicide in the stables has been seen in a house built on the grounds. In the main house, a woman in grey makes noises, screams, talking and even practical jokes.

Making quite a change from the usual horse and rider or even phantom coach stories, a ghostly motorbike has been heard pulling up outside the police station, where footsteps in an empty corridor and a door that refused to stay closed have been reported.

Ghost rang bells at Poolway House, Gloucester Road.

Speech House hotel and restaurant is where the Verderers, who were responsible for looking after the King's interests in the Forest of Dean, originally held their court. A quiet lady walks at midnight through the house. A horseman, carrying his head in his hands and sometimes riding his horse around the grounds.

Roundheads have been sighted at Whitecliff House in Whitecliff near Coleford, also poltergeist activity, perhaps by a child.

Compton Abdale

A horse and trap, bearing lights, has regularly been seen near Hangman's Stone, at the crossroads on the A40 from Salperton to Compton Abdale. Also on the A40, invisible stage coaches pull up outside the Puesdown Inn where a ghost horse and rider, perhaps a local highwayman called The Duke who died here during an escape attempt, hammers on the front door. Footsteps heard going across the lounge and up the stairs; someone or something clanks chains.

Cranham

Eddel, a British chieftain before the Saxon invasion, died of poison at Cranham and was buried at what is known as Eddel's Tump. Said to still haunt the woods and lanes near the Tump and Eddel's Mill.

Deerhurst

Woman in Edwardian clothes seen in 1968 walking up the path to the Saxon St Mary's church before disappearing.

Dodington

Piano playing heard in Dodington House, possibly the ghost of Lady Georgiana Codrington who died in 1881. Other mysterious happenings at the house, such as taps turning themselves on and doors opening and shutting by themselves, prompted Bath spiritualist Philip Steff and three other mediums from the Bath Psychic Club to hold a seance in the cellar in July 1980. During this, Steff said he made contact with 'an unhappy coloured stable lad from the 17th century.'

Dovers Hill

Lady in white cloak seen at the foot of the hill, said to be a girl called Beatrice, from a Puritan family, whose lover, a Royalist highwayman, was murdered here by her brothers.

Dursley

Numerous hauntings have been reported at The Old Bell Hotel in Long Street, by the ghost of a chambermaid who hanged herself in room 6 after being made pregnant and then abandoned by her boyfriend.

Eastleach Martin

In a field called Crossways, the ghost of a very tall man was often seen at night, carrying his head under his arm. In the middle of the last century, the field was drained and a stone coffin was discovered. When the lid was removed, the skeleton of a tall man was exposed – his skull was under his arm. The bones turned to dust on exposure to the air. The tenant at the farm, a Charles Barton, took the teeth, which were well preserved, and it is said carried them about in his waistcoat pocket before eventually burying them.

At a house called The Peacocks, a ghost haunted a particular room until some children decided to play in it. Their boisterous play caused something to drop down onto the floor. It was described as 'a knob of gold.' After this, the ghost was not seen again.

Edge

In a field on Edge Farm called Hanging Hill a farmhand, said to have hanged himself after losing a bet to mow the whole field in one day, can be heard still scything the grass. A Roman centurion was seen by a local policeman near the site of a Roman villa on Haresfield Hill.

Flaxley

A small grey figure has been seen at night in meadows around this hamlet near Cinderford. Thought to be Wulfram, an 80-year old monk who refused to leave Flaxley Abbey when it was destroyed during the Dissolution and hid himself away in a secret room, only going out at night to forage for food. Monks also seen working in the woods. Sue Law in *More Ghosts of the Forest of Dean*, relates a story told to her by a motorcyclist who, in 1982 on the Flaxley road just past the abbey, followed a ghostly stag into fields where it disappeared.

Frocester

Ghost of an old lady prevented one of the bells in the redundant church being removed.

Dodington House, where mysterious happenings have been witnessed.

A ghost of a cavalier has been said to knock on the door of the Angel Hotel, Coleford.

Gatcombe

Sir Francis Drake often stayed at Gatcombe, a small hamlet near Blakeney, when he was in the Forest of Dean supervising timber for his ships. Local tradition has it that his ghost has been seen sitting staring down the Severn. The question begs to be asked – why should the great mariner haunt here rather than the many other places with much more substantial associations?

Gloucester

ARCHDEACON STREET SCHOOL, (now part of College of Technology): Haunted in the late 1960s by a teacher who had died there.

BEARLAND HOUSE: Lady in white.

LACKFRIARS: 13th century Dominican priory. Monk; friar with blood pouring from his head running from the nave.

LLANTHONY ROAD: Archaeologists occupying the Old Bridge Inn while excavating the North Gate of the city in 1974 heard strange noises – scratching, banging etc – in the night. Two murders said to have taken place there. A figure of man has also been seen in a tool shop in Llanthony Road.

CATHEDRAL: There is a legend that when the cathedral was being built a 14-year old apprentice fell off the scaffolding and died. His ghost had to be exorcised and his spirit was placed in a jar which was buried in one of the huge pillars. A face has been seen at the window of a room in St Mary's Gate, looking down on the spot where Protestant Bishop John Hooper was burned at the stake on February 9th 1555. The suggestion is that the watcher is Queen Mary and that she had travelled in secret to the city to make sure that her orders had been carried out.

DOCKS: When one of the old warehouses was being converted into a restaurant a few years ago, a lot of poltergeist activity was recorded. A ghost ship with two bodies hanging from the yard arm has been seen in the docks.

FLEECE HOTEL: Elizabethan lady in blue dress passes through door to the building next door (once a gentlemen's club) and in the corridors.

GLOUCESTER JAIL: Ghost of Jenny Godfrey, murdered here by a drunken Irishman in the 15th century when an abbey stood on this site. Reports of furniture in cell 25 on landing A3 being moved happened over many years. In 1969 the occupant of Cell 25, Robert Gore, and other prisoners held a seance during which Jenny communicated through an upturned glass. After that pots, pans, books etc were thrown around the cell, and a few days later a disembodied hand appeared and pointed its index finger straight at Gore.

GREAT WESTERN HOSPITAL: Soldier in WWI uniform.

GREYFRIARS INN: Moving furniture, loud noises, doors opening, lights being switched on and off etc.

INNER COURT WINE BAR, Southgate Street: Playful poltergeist wobbles tables, topples glasses and creates cold chills. Manageress Mrs Jane Gage in 1985 told the *Western Daily Press* 'Most of us now joke about it. We have got used to having it around and never know what's going to happen next.'

KINGSBARTON THEATRE: With all the passion generated on stage, most theatres (and indeed many cinemas) have their own ghosts, often of famous actors and actresses who have starred there. The Gloucester Operatic and Dramatic Society (GODS) put on their productions in this converted Salvation Army Citadel from 1963 until they opened the New Olympus Theatre in 1985. Many of their members have heard footsteps walking across the stage and the ghost of a man was once seen. It's been suggested that the building is haunted either by a Salvation Army captain or a man who committed suicide in a meat factory that was on this site before it became the Citadel.

KINGSHOLM INN: Poltergeist activity and a ghost, possibly a previous publican.

RUSSELL STREET: Girl of about seven years old in Victorian dress, man in old fashioned mourning clothes, child singing etc in building housing insurance office. The staff of the office carried out detailed research of the history of the house and their findings are related in full in Eileen Fry's *Strange and Ghostly Tales of Historic Gloucester*. A medium contacted Agnes Nancy Wingate, a deaf and dumb child who had died here aged seven years; the man was her uncle Edwin Wingate (born 1825) headmaster of a school in Russell Street.

STROUD ROAD: Another unusual story told by Eileen Fry relates to a seance in a furniture restorer's workshop (since moved to the Antique Centre in the Docks). Contact was made with a young boy who, with his mother, died after being trapped in a burning house during the Civil War. The house and its neighbours along the outside of the city walls were set alight by Roundhead soldiers in case Royalist troops used them for shelter.

TEWKESBURY ROAD: New houses have been built on the corner of Estcourt Road, once a children's hospital (Gambier Parry Lodge) run by nuns. Legend says that one of the young nuns hanged herself after the death of a baby in her care and her ghostly figure remained to walk the corridors of the Lodge, usually with the baby in her arms. The sound of a crying baby was regularly heard. During demolition, the builders were so wary that they worked in pairs.

THEATRE ROYAL: Numbers 28–34 Westgate Street, occupied by a Poundstretcher store and the offices of the Nationwide Anglia building society are on the site of the former Theatre Royal. In 1976, the *Gloucester Citizen* carried a story that the ghost of lady in a grey dress had been seen on the staircase of the DIY store then occupying this site. It is thought that the site was haunted by the ghost of Eliza Johnson who, in 1880, committed suicide in the theatre. The letter E (presumably Eliza again) has also appeared on a wall in the cellar.

TUFFLEY AVENUE: A large number of very unusual events recorded in a gothic style Victorian house in Tuffley Avenue, including electrical goods being switched on, footsteps, the telephone being dialled and left off the hook and the owner's two dogs being strangled. Owner in 1987 said there were four or five spirits in the house. Vicar of St Barnabus, Gloucester, the Rev Tony Minchin, performed a communion service to settle the spirits.

WESTGATE STREET: Man with long white hair, beard, grey robe haunted the office of Anglian Windows in Westgate Street in 1988. Carpet lifted, furniture thrown. Seance revealed it was the ghost of a man who had died after falling from the building. Perfumed lady in basement of a shop on the corner of Westgate and St John's Lane. The ghost of a girl haunts the Dick Whittington public house, said to be of a servant girl who died in 1604 from the plague. An assistant manageress must have upset her when she went into one room because all the glasses was thrown from the wall. A man was seen walking through a wall by a workman during renovations and a carpenter in 1982 was working alone in the cellar and had one of his tools passed to him by an unseen person. Present landlord says that his dog occasionally emits a low growl in an upstairs room for no discernible reason.

Goodrich

Ghostly shrieks of a young couple, Alice Birch (Parliament) and her lover Charles Clifford (Cavalier) who escaped together from the Siege of Goodrich Castle in the Civil War but died trying to cross the River Wye.

Hambrook

There's a friendly mischief-making ghost at the Hambrook Inn who switches electrical appliances on, moves things about etc.

Hanham Abbots

The church in the grounds of Hanham Court haunted by a woman in white, a nun perhaps. At Court Farm, a man was seen going into the barn where he disappeared.

Idbury

On the Oxfordshire border with Gloucestershire. A haunted wood, well known amongst gypsies for ghosts that they called 'Snow Foresters'.

Kempsford

Grey lady walks on the surface of the Thames at Kempsford. Said to be Lady Maud Plantaganet who in the 13th century was thrown in the river to drown by her husband Henry Plantaganet, Earl of Lancaster. St Mary's Vicarage was once claimed to be one of Britain's most haunted houses, with a veritable army of ghosts, including a disembodied hand, a frightened mother, a silent monk and a boy in lace and breeches. In 1986 a man in black walked from one of the bedrooms and straight through a wall.

Leonard Stanley

Hooded monk haunts the churchyard.

Littledean

According to a local story, one house in this Forest of Dean village was so haunted that nobody would sleep in it or even walk near it. It was eventually pulled down. The local story is that a couple living there committed suicide and killed their child when it was discovered that they were brother and sister living incestuously.

CHURCH FARM: Grey lady. 17th century farmhouse.

LITTLEDEAN HALL: Claims to be England's oldest house and one of its most haunted houses. Numerous ghosts have been sighted here, as well as footsteps, and poltergeist activity, including the ghost of a black servant who murdered his master, a ghostly gardener, blood stains, a white monk and a lady in yellow.

RED HOUSE: Man walks through the gate in tall black hat, perhaps a Quaker for they used Red House as a Meeting House.

LITTLEDEAN HOUSE HOTEL: Man in large velvet cap and long cape.

LITTLEDEAN GRANGE: Noises, shadows and shapes heard in the ruins plus a frightening white mist. Ghost rider and horse.

LITTLEDEAN JAIL: Door opened by itself, even though locked and bolted.

SILVER STREET: Platoon of Roman soldiers.

GUN MILLS: Bent figure carrying a sack on its back; monks at St Anthony's Well, once a place of pilgrimage for its curative properties.

GREENBOTTOM: Village on the other side of Welshbury Woods to Flaxley, the ghost of deformed boy who had been kept hidden by his mother, escaped and died in the woods unable to fend for himself.

Lydbrook

BET KEBIR: Ghost of a man descending the staircase in riding habit. In an old cottage by the railway line a girl is said to have thrown herself from an upstairs window and still haunts the area. She was a miner's daughter who fell in love with a man who thought himself too good for her.

Lydney

On July 22nd, 1771 William Morgan murdered Miss Jones of Naas House while trying to rob her and her companion Miss Gough near Lydney Church. Morgan, in stove pipe hat, cape and thigh boots has subsequently been sighted in the Naas Lane area. Sue Law in *Ghosts of the Forest of Dean* tells of another interesting sighting near Naas House, of a similarly clothed body hanging by its neck from a tree. Three monks have been seen walking down the middle of Driffield Road.

Maisemore

The White Hart has experienced a lot of unusual activity. Bottles and glasses have been thrown around the bar, the juke box has been turned on, there have been bangs and tapping and a sighting in the cellar.

Mickleton

Sir Edward Greville, who owned huge sections of Gloucestershire in the 16th century had one son, but one night he accidently shot the boy dead in mistake for a robber. Where this sad event took place has become known as Weeping Hollow because of Sir Edward's grief. The boy's ghost is heard rather than seen and known locally as the Mickleton Hooter or Belhowja because of the noise it makes. Sir Edward sold his land and the village in 1597.

Minchinhampton

Ghostly coach and horses seen driving up Well Hill. Phantom black dog near Long Stone, a standing stone with holes through which children were passed as a cure for whooping cough. The stone is said to move around the field at midnight of its own accord.

Mitcheldean

Eli Hatton was convicted of murdering Tom Turberville in Mitcheldean in 1732. His ghost appears at Pingry Tump, where his body was hung in chains on the gibbet after he was hanged.

Moreton-in-Marsh

The Manor House Hotel, formerly Creswyke House, said to be haunted by the ghost of Dame Creswyke, who drowned in a pool in the 18th century.

Nailsworth

Ghostly figure seen sitting on a bench by the roadside in the lane from Nailsworth to Box.

Newland

Civil War cavaliers and a ghostly coach sighted in the village. A woman and a baby in her arms seen emerging from Swan Pool on the Newland to Redbrook road. A sinister black dog also seen.

Newnham-on-Severn

Parts of the Victoria Hotel date back to 1550, but its ghost is only from the 19th century: a chambermaid, Annie, who was thwarted in love and hanged herself in the attic haunts the top landings. Woman in grey seen on the river bank.

Oakle Street

A new bungalow in this village near Churcham subjected to a host of poltergeist activity, including 40 fires. In 1991 a psychic told the owners their house was built on burial place for 10th century monks and nuns burned to death.

Oakridge

Headless riders reported seen near Golden Coffin Field and Money Tump, both remains of long barrows. As the names of the barrows suggest some form of hidden treasure, it has been suggested that the hauntings may have been invented by field owners to keep away treasure hunters while they themselves searched for anything that may have been hidden here.

Over

Ghost of a woman who committed suicide by drowning herself in the fish pond, seen at Over Court on December 17th; the anniversary of her death, rising from the pond.

Painswick

There's a royal ghost at The Court House – Charles I who haunts the building in which he ordered the siege of Gloucester. Ghostly Cavaliers have also been seen in both the grounds and garden, presumably preparing for the siege. The cellars of the Little Fleece Inn, which dates from the 14th century, haunted by the ghost of a former owner hunting for buried treasure.

Postlip

An exorcism was held in the gabled Postlip Hall at the turn of the century by the chaplain of the chapel in the manor grounds. The nature of the haunting is not known.

Poulton

Betty's Grave at Poulton between Cirencester and Fairford marks the burial place of Elizabeth Bastre who died in 1786. Various stories have been linked with Betty, whose grave is now such a prominent feature of the landscape it is marked on Ordnance Survey maps. One story is that she was a witch who poisoned herself, or was hanged for witchcraft (or sheepstealing) and was buried here to confuse her spirit so it wouldn't know which road to take. It obviously worked, because her ghost still haunts the crossroads. Alternative stories relate that she was a local woman who died of exposure after betting a man that she could mow a field (or hoe a field of turnips) faster than him, or that she was a servant who was murdered by her master.

Prestbury

A black Abbot seen at Easter, Christmas and All Saints' Day walking from the church, through the churchyard to 16th century Reform Cottage in Deep Street whose garden is on burial ground of the Priory. A 'leering' monk has also been seen in the town.

The ghost of a Royalist dispatch rider travelling from the battle of Worcester to Gloucester or perhaps to Tewkesbury in 1471 with news of the fighting, gallops through the Burgage and Mill Lane. A knight in armour on horseback was also seen in the Burgage area and another story tells of a horse being heard in a courtyard of a house in the same area, the rider dismounting and entering the house. In the 1970s two plumbers working in the house saw the figure of an old man with a long white beard who waved his stick at them and shouted to them to 'Get Out'.

An old lady in old-fashioned clothes peers into windows of buildings in the main high street and disappears by the almshouses built by Ann Goodrich in 1720. Another old lady in a big hat, a singing ghost, a servant girl in long dress and mop cap and even a jockey in peaked cap, racing blouse and breeches.

SUNDIAL COTTAGE: Ghost of former resident, a music professor or a young girl depending on stories, plays the spinet.

WALNUT COTTAGE: Old Moses, perhaps an evil racehorse owner or a groom from the 18th century. When challenged by a former owner, the ghost replied 'Here's Old Moses. You see I likes to look in sometimes.'

SWINDON LANE: Shepherd and ghostly sheep seen on a foggy night in 1975.

IDSALL HOUSE: Man pushed from behind in the basement (now offices) when there was no one else in the room.

CLEEVE CORNER: Old house near the church, part of which accommodated the monks of Llanthony Priory. People have felt they were being strangled. A young bride was murdered in the cottage by a thief.

MILL STREET: Lots of sightings here – of a legless man, white lady, an old lady gathering wood and the sound of marching men.

OLD RACE COURSE: Vanishing man and more interestingly, an old fashioned funeral cortège, with black plumed horses and mourners in black clothes seen crossing a field.

BOUNCER'S LANE: Ghostly gardener seen at work on the allotments.

Ruardean

Pantod Mine on top of Ruardean Hill was haunted by either an owner who was thrown down the shaft by his men because he refused to pay them their rightful wages or a drunken stone mason. A bundle of rags and bones were found in the mine.

At 9.30am every Monday morning, the kitchen door to a house in the village was opened. The owner felt a gentle breeze flow through the kitchen across the sitting room and up the stairs but never a sighting.

St Briavels

A phantom fiddler has been heard in the lanes of this Forest of Dean village. St Briavels Castle, now a youth hostel, is haunted by at least three ghosts: a man in armour, a lady in white and a man in centuries old costume. The ghost of a young girl called Emmaline whose father had arranged that she marry an older man despite the fact that she loved another, haunts Cinderhill House. On her wedding day she ran out of the church in the middle of the service, down Cinderhill to the well into which she jumped and drowned. Footsteps have been heard along the upstairs corridor of The George Inn.

Sharpness

Near a former railway bridge is a whirlpool called Fiddlers Pool. A party of Welsh fiddlers rowed across to play in a pub in Berkeley. They drunk too much on the journey back, their boat overturned and they were drowned. On stormy nights the sound of fiddles is heard.

Sheepscombe

Anne Boleyn and Henry VIII, who hunted here, have been seen in Sheepscombe Woods.

Sherborne

Ghost walks the Monk's Passage in Sherborne House, while at Lodge Park House, John 'Crump' Dutton, a keen gambler, is said to have been seen driving a coach and horses towards the house, which was built as a hunting and coursing lodge.

Shipton Oliffe

At the Frogmore Inn, an old man, young girl and child seen sitting at a table in one of the bedrooms playing cards. Whispering also heard.

Staverton

An old soldier and a maid haunt the 15th century Pheasant Inn. Heavy footsteps and locked doors.

Stoke Bishop

Stoke House in this fashionable suburb of Bristol, formerly in Gloucestershire, was built by wealthy Bristol merchant Sir Robert Cannin 1669. It was one of his relatives who, under the impression that his daughter's lover was climbing a tree outside her bedroom window, mistakenly shot and killed her instead as she was about to elope. She is said to have haunted the passages of Stoke House ever since.

Stow on the Wold

In 1963 – 64, a semi-detached house in Chapen Street was subjected to a whole host of poltergeist activity. A small boy watching the television and an old lady seated in an armchair have been seen at The King's Arms Hotel. The Royalist Hotel in Digbeth Street is one of the oldest inns in the country (the timbers used in the building's frame were radio-carbon date-tested and found to be more than 1,000 years old) so it is to be expected that there should be ghost stories attached to it. One room has a particularly bad atmosphere; two children are said to have been starved to death in the building – perhaps it was in this room?

Stroud

Stage coach has been seen on the narrow road from Minchinhampton Common to Woodchester. Footsteps and cries heard in the old Stroud Union Workhouse building in Bisley Road, but only in early morning along the corridor leading to the main section of the building.

Sudeley

Ghost of Prince Rupert's hunting dog, killed in the first siege of Sudeley Castle where his master had his headquarters. Janet, a former housekeeper, dressed in white blouse, long pink and white skirt, mob-cap, seen in various bedrooms.

Syde

A white coach drawn by four white horses seen on Ermine Way (A417) by the turn-off to Syde in 1972.

Tetbury

The ubiquitous lady in grey has been seen at Chavenage Manor as well as a monk in the chapel, perhaps from the vanished Horsley priory which seems to have supplied the house with some of its windows and other features. More interesting is the ghost of a man in uniform, not a Cavalier or Roundhead as is common in Gloucestershire, but a South American-looking man with long black hair and a Viva Zapata style moustache. Ghost of owner Nathaniel Stephens and headless Charles I seen on former's burial day.

Old lady seen doing the ironing in The Talbot. Lady in blue dress in the Trouble Inn at Cherington on the Cirencester road.

Tewkesbury

A monk leaves the Abbey through the West door and walks in the direction of the vicarage. Another, in a black habit, has been seen walking inside the abbey and then climbs up an invisible staircase before vanishing. A white lady has been sighted in the churchyard.

After the top floor of the 15th century Berkeley Arms in Church Street was sealed off, tapping sounds and footsteps were heard. In 1974 the wall that blocked off the area was removed – but the sounds continued. A headless man drags a chain in the Black Bear and an old woman sits in the corner of the bar. In the Tudor House Hotel in High Street, a black labrador dog has been seen on the landing of the main stairs and a white lady goes upstairs into a first floor bedroom, glides across the room before vanishing.

Thornbury

A phantom 'bottom pincher' was reported at The Exchange Hotel (now The Knot of Rope) in the 1960s, nicknamed 'Charlie' by regulars. Glasses thrown from tables, doors slammed by themselves, beer casks rumbled across the empty cellar floor. At one time, the number of visitations stood at 46.

Thrupp

Nether Lypiatt Manor, the home of Prince and Princess Michael of Kent, haunted by the ghost of the blacksmith who made the wrought iron gates, by a frock-coated man seated at the dining table, a grey lady and a woman in white.

Uckington

A ghostly curse was blamed by villagers in 1987 for a string of problems they experienced when trying to move a memorial, commemorating the fallen of Uckington and Elmstone Hardwicke, into the parish church. A Bristol mason who offered to do the job fell off a church tower and broke his wrist and some ribs.

Uley

In the Second World War evacuees at Owlpen Manor were kissed goodnight by a lady in a sumptuous red dress, pointed hat and veil. Said to be the ghost of Margaret of Anjou, wife of Henry VI. Also said to be haunted by a Black Monk who, according to local legend, was walled up and starved to death by the owners after fleeing the sacking of Kingswood Abbey.

Westbury-on-Severn

Lady in a grey crinoline dress sits on the window seat at the top of the stairs of a house on the outskirts of the village.

Wigpool

Woman in white seen near Wigpool pond, presumably someone who once drowned herself there. Voices heard whispering in the old Wigpool iron mines.

Winchcombe

Meredith in his *The Haunted Cotswolds* gives information about two haunted houses in Winchcombe. In the first, a house in the centre of the town, a woman in old-fashioned nurse's costume has been seen, as well as a great deal of poltergeist activity – rattling doorknobs, moving household objects, water gushing from taps that have been turned off etc. In a house on the other side of town there's an old woman with long white hair in plaits with a pockmarked face and wearing a lace wedding dress. Behind the figure could be seen the outline of a trench that, according to Meredith's informant, seemed to run right through the kitchen wall.

A monk floats two feet above the ground in the vicinity of the abbey ruins, usually, it is said, before a local tragedy. Ghostly choir also reported. The Mill Inn is haunted by the ghost of a landlady who drowned in the River Coln, while The Old Corner Cupboard Inn has phantom monks (part of the ancient inn is on the site of the old monastery) and the sound of a young child. A monk has also been seen near the old station and at Pyke Bank. A family picnicking on Belas Tump, a long barrow on Cleeve Common, saw their laden table cloth fly into the air, throwing food, crockery etc all over the place.

A cyclist riding in Margrett's Hollow found that his bike just wouldn't move, even though when he checked it over there was nothing mechanically wrong with it. In the end he had to physically drag it along the road.

Winterbourne

A cottage on Winterbourne Down near the old quarry is haunted by a man, possibly someone injured in an accident at the workings who was brought to the cottage where he died.

Withington

The Mill Inn has been haunted by a veiled lady, perhaps the elderly woman who according to local stories drowned in the nearby river, two men and an old couple in the bar.

Woodchester

A number of ghosts are said to haunt Woodchester Park and were investigated by Geoff Bird of the Associations for the Scientific Study of Anomalous Phenomena (ASSAP). They include a headless Centurion, ragged dwarf, a floating coffin which hovers over a lake and the ghosts of two American servicemen. A black dog heralded imminent death of a Dominican.

Wotton-under-Edge

The former Ram Inn, now a private house, has a host of ghosts, including a cavalier, a lady called Elizabeth, Tom the Tramp, one or two monks and a shepherd. There has also been a lot of poltergeist activity – one visitor was thrown out of bed – and a strong presence.

Further Reading

Abdy-Collins, B., *The Cheltenham Ghost* (Psychic Press 1948)

Alexander, Marc, *Haunted Inns* (Frederick Muller, 1973)

Bord, Janet and Colin, *Atlas of Magical Britain* (Sidgwick & Jackson, 1990)

Briggs, Katharine M., *The Folklore of the Cotswolds* (B.T. Batsford 1974)

Brooks, J.A., *Ghosts and Witches of the Cotswolds* (Jarrolds 1981)

Cohen, Daniel, *The Encyclopaedia of Ghosts* (Michael O'Mara Books 1989)

Fry, Eileen, *Strange and Ghostly Tales of Historic Gloucester* (Architext Publns, 1989)

Green, Andrew, *Our Haunted Kingdom* (Wolfe 1973)

Hallam, Jack, *The Haunted Inns of England* (Wolfe 1972)

Law, Sue, *Ghosts of the Forest of Dean* (Forest Bookshop 1982)

Law, Sue, *More Ghosts of the Forest of Dean* (Forest Bookshop, 1991)

Maple, Eric, *Supernatural England* (Robert Hale 1977)

Meredith, Bob, *Cheltenham: Town of Shadows* (Reardon & Son, 1988)

Peach, Emily, *Things that go bump in the night* (Aquarian Press 1991)

Playfair, Guy Lyon, *The Haunted Pub Guide* (Harrap 1985)

Royal, Margaret and Girvan, Ian, *Bristol Ghosts and their Neighbours* (Abson Books 1977)

Ryder, T.A., *Lore and Legend of Gloucestershire* (1989 Manuscript only, in Gloucester Reference Library)

Sale, Richard, *A Visitor's Guide to the Cotswolds* (Moorland Publishing, 1982)

Smith, Betty, *Tales of Old Gloucestershire* (Countryside Books, 1987)

Underwood, Peter, *Ghostly Encounters* (Bossiney Books, 1991)